Stanley Beavan grew up in Herefordshire, where he currently lives with his wife and two sons. The author loves life, maximising a successful working career and a fun social life to the full. When confronted with stage IV cancer diagnosis at the age of 44, Stanley adopted a determined strategy anchored by positivity and drawing on life's experience and energy of those around him to defeat the disease.

The Complete Response charts Stanley's incredible journey from diagnosis to full recovery against the odds. Stanley remains free of cancer.

This book is dedicated to all those who are faced with a major life event or diagnosis, I hope this read helps. It is also dedicated to those who gave me love and support through an incredibly difficult journey, especially my wife and sons.

Stanley Beavan

THE COMPLETE
RESPONSE

From Stage 4 Cancer to Full Recovery

AUSTIN MACAULEY PUBLISHERS™

LONDON • CAMBRIDGE • NEW YORK • SHARJAH

A CIP catalogue record for this title is available from the British Library.

ISBN 9781528938259 (Paperback)
ISBN 9781528938266 (Hardback)
ISBN 9781528969482 (ePub e-book)

www.austinmacauley.com

First Published (2020)
Austin Macauley Publishers Ltd
25 Canada Square
Canary Wharf
London
E14 5LQ

Introduction

We are, in fact, all dying, some will take many decades but for some, it is sooner, just around the corner. Most of us take life for granted, ignoring the one certain thing in life, death. Even if you outlive the predicted time when you were supposed to die by one minute more, it is a positive, every second we breathe is so precious especially when we stop to appreciate what is around us. Love Life!

During our lifetime, we take so much for granted, health, the people around us and sometimes remain totally immune from major life changing events like death, divorce, disease or life-threatening illness or financial disasters. How we are each individually geared as humans will define how we respond to such events which often come without warning and turn an otherwise routine and regular lifestyle on its head.

The ability to adapt the mind from day one is key, setting the tone for how you deal with this event, engaging the right set of principles, getting through the shock or news and 'adapting', developing a strategy is so important. Drawing down on the potential you have as an individual, syncing into anything positive that makes you feel good and taking the best expert advice you can take where needed and sticking to tight regimes whether they be medical, regular doses of positivity or new changes like diet. Feeding off positive past experiences and knowing who you are as an individual are critical.

Accept change, it will happen to all of us and embrace it as actually the stark reality of life. Adapt and look for your mental potential to overcome, accept and deal with the harder side of life. I believe, we are all able to unlock certain parts of our brain and select the right gear when needed. If you are able to build a fantastic support network, use the people around you to move forward and develop focuses which will give you positive releases, you can then tackle most of what life throws at you. Take ownership, take responsibility and take control.

Whatever you have to confront, is a challenge and like training for a sporting event, like say a marathon, you have to condition yourself to want to meet the challenge in stages, day by day overcoming hurdles, obstacles and channelling your inner energy and focus. You are already a born fighter, as half egg, half sperm, you have already been winning races before you were born.

This is simply an insight into my life and one man's approach to one of life's curve balls and the way I sought to deal with it and still deal with it. If it can help just one more person facing a major life event then I am smiling already.

It is ultimately up to you if you accept the need to adapt and develop a positive mental attitude to overcome a major life event. Enjoy the ride if you do, it can make you appreciate things a lot more and especially the things we take for granted all around us. Be strong, be positive and even if you don't win against life's challenges, take positivity that you gave it your best shot.

Chapter 1
Get Ready for Change

Briefly looking down at his notes, Dr Amos then looked up and at me, staring sternly straight into my eyes and said with a low matter of fact tone, "The bowel biopsies have come back suspicious of cancer but are not conclusive, but in my view, this looks to be a cancer, upper rectal or recto-sigmoid cancer."

I remained silent for a moment trying to detect any empathy in his voice and then politely responded in as calm a voice I could muster, "How aggressive, on a scale of 1–3?"

He paused, looked right into my eyes for a second time, still with a serious expression, and said, "A stage 4." I thought for a second or two, gradually processing this news and its impact on my day, but all I could think of was the fact I hadn't given him 1–4 options, only options 1–3.

Before I could think any further with my train of thought he continued, "The scan also showed some black spots on either side of your liver which would indicate that, if it is, indeed, an aggressive cancer, it has unfortunately had time to spread. The bowel and liver are closely linked and the liver is one of the major organs bowel cancer can spread to. I would recommend you see an oncologist right away." I was just sat there listening and processing, absorbing but strategizing in my mind at the same time…one of the things I thought was, *what the fuck is an oncologist?*

Somewhere in my brain, a voice was saying this is different, you do risk, like challenge, we will attack it…but this is as big as they come.

Chapter 2
Anaglypta – Summer 1990

Do It All Hereford (the City's newest DIY store), was my first job aged 18, a weekend job while studying at sixth form. I was still a skinny teenager, 5ft 10, spotty and self-conscious and I really didn't want to work but I needed money to sustain my nights out and desire to impress women with my random fashion sense. Word of mouth had spread that they were looking for students to do weekend shifts and this suited a few of the guys I knew from sixth form, for a bit of extra petrol and beer money. Give or take a few weeks, we all started broadly at the same time, enduring endless lectures on health and safety, things like pricing of paint, tutorials on mixing paint and of course customer care. Possibly the most outrageous thing was the uniform, the bright blue dungarees we all had to wear with a loud rainbow embroidered in the centre of your chest (not the most fashionable outfit for the image-conscious student trying to impress the chicks!)

I had ended up assigned to the garden centre section, mainly based outside, endlessly watering plants, rearranging grow bags and fence panels, slabs, pansies and the like. My pal, TJ, had ended up on an indoor job advising on drills and anything electronic, whilst Digger, another pal and the scrawny but brains of the trio, had ended up on the customer service desk (they saw him as potential management material). Clearly, they had us sussed out perfectly well in the right order, from the moment we walked in.

From day one, Digger took his job far too seriously, he took pleasure in calling the rest of us to run errands over the store's loud customer announcement tannoy system, regularly exercising his new found authoritative voice, calling us at his liberty to attend to customer wants and needs. I was, however, very happy, I preferred the freedom of not being stuck inside a building and enjoyed most aspects of the garden centre apart from dropping the occasional patio slab on my foot. Plus, I couldn't hear so much of the tannoy announcements, so I had a good excuse not to be available to run errands for the service desk all of the time.

It was, perhaps, a defining moment when one particular Saturday, I ran out of patience with Digger, following his repeated request for TJ and I to attend the warehouse section of the store located behind the main retail sales area and locate a roll of Anaglypta wallpaper for a customer. No doubt, some pensioner was looking to liven up their hallway and suffer the tricky consequences of getting this product off the wall 30 years later! If they were still alive, that is!

I met TJ exiting his aisle of shiny drills, also en route to the warehouse and who looked as pissed off as I was, I was muttering under my breath that Digger had, yet again, called me away from the more interesting task of watering my prized pansies and catching the afternoon sunshine.

From his comfy chair behind the customer service desk, in the nice warm store, Digger knew 1) that the only box of Anaglypta was 30 feet up the warehouse racking (he could tell that from his computer screen), 2) I was not the biggest fan of heights, 3) that he would keep raising the customer request over the tannoy for all to hear including our managers, until we retrieved the roll and presented it to the customer who was waiting patiently at the service desk. Digger had very little physicality to his job.

The warehouse was, as usual, very cold and we didn't have the usual 15-foot wheel ladder that I fondly remembered from the Do It All health and safety video tutorial briefings on working at height. So the two of us threw the rule book out of the window and proceeded to climb up the shelves of the racking, ignoring our health and safety training, aware of the frequent tannoy announcements (Digger was clearly losing patience, as I imagine was the elderly customer stood next to him). Going up the racking for me had not been an option I relished, it took time to battle my fear but eventually, we reached a dusty box six shelves up from the ground. I was feeling queasy, dizzy and the racking wasn't made for climbing the way I did it, like a nervous cat clinging onto a tree trunk for dear life, inching slowly upwards! It took me time to acclimatise to my new surroundings, a flat slatted wooden shelf with restricted head height and an assortment of boxed shrink-wrapped home decoration items and a load of grow bags. TJ, however, was a lot more confident, like Spiderman on steroids in fact, reaching the shelf with ease and immediately opening the gaffa-taped box of wallpaper with his Stanley knife, out of puff, we both proceeded to peer in.

"Here we go," he exclaimed, "Do It All's best rolls of wallpaper—Anaglypta!"

It was at that moment Digger walked into the warehouse oblivious to our exact location, authoritatively with his hands on his hips as he paused to survey the quiet warehouse and vast array of shelved or palleted DIY products, scrutinising every corner for a few seconds at a time, longing to one day be able to slip out of his dungarees and into a suit only worn by a member of the management team. Digger had no idea where we were in the warehouse, albeit he knew it was on a high shelf but given we were both hidden on a section of racking obscured by a pallet of grow bags, he couldn't see us.

I heard him clearly say, "Where are those lazy bastards?" at which point I instinctively took out a second roll of Anaglypta from the box and muttered under my breath, "Here's your roll of Anaglypta, tannoy man!" and threw it at him. There was a loud smack…yes, I heard a *smack*, then the next few seconds were a blur of…well reality, slight regret, fear of getting down to assess the damage, the damage to Do It All's first line of defence against a throng of customers I imagined were now queuing angrily at the customer service desk.

The first thing TJ said was, "Shit, mate, I think you have killed him! He went down like a sack of spuds, you got him right on the back of his head!"

I had never knowingly tried to kill someone and it concerned me at that moment with that gut wrenching wish to reverse a wrong that I had felt as a kid. I thought this is serious, I am in trouble here with no escape route, I was thinking, would the police be called? It took me a while to get down again confronting my fear of heights but I was embracing my fear with more courage, the shock of having cut short the life of potential Do It All management material slightly more my new focus. My stomach was in my mouth as I descended the racking, my mouth bone dry.

Fortunately or unfortunately, whichever way you look at it, I hadn't decided at the time, Digger was sat upright by the time I got down, swearing at me and clutching the back of his head, "…What the fuck happened?" he exclaimed, unable to get to his feet.

Stammering for words, I made out the roll fell out of my hands due to my fear of heights and that it wasn't intended to be aimed at him, I am not sure he was 100% convinced at that exact time, he would one day understand me better. As we lifted him to his feet and walked him to the staff room past the throngs of customers looking pissed off with having to wait, TJ and I managed to exchange a grin. I trusted TJ, I was learning he was dependable when I was in difficulty. It had been a close shave with risk but I kind of felt relief, elation and a taste for more all at the same time.

These days, Digger sees that incident as the first of three attempts by me to kill him (I will get around to telling you about the other two later) and he has sought revenge several times since, never letting me forget those incidents. This episode, however, captured a sense of the type of person I was—a risk taker, looking for the higher plain of fun and pursuit of the life less ordinary and unbeknown to me, the Do It All event would lead to the birth of the Anaglypta Club in 2016.

I walked away from the incident knowing that somewhere inside me, be it my brain or soul, I was definitely a risk taker and sometimes living along the edge…the untamed Maverick, I just needed to know how to control it, how to channel it. I loved the feeling of risk but I wasn't weighing up the consequences, I needed to be able to adapt whatever the bad news, deal psychologically with the shock of the moment. I had nearly killed someone!

Chapter 3
The Horny Hound, 2016

It was early January 2016, I had been sat at my desk slightly bored with the morning's work so I emailed Larry Branagan, a private art dealer, based a mile or so from where my office was located, for a beer/chat at lunchtime. Larry embraced life's rich tapestry, living life to the full especially when it came to the ladies. I agreed we would rendezvous at a small quiet bar between where our respective offices were located, grab a table and chill out having a catch up. Larry was in his early 50s but looked as if he was in his mid-40s, a fit five foot nine muscular build, with an unrivalled well-mannered gift of the gab when it came to women. Larry was a good art dealer who bought and sold mainly abstract art and had a lovely way with people. Larry was, however, either up or down having had deep episodes of depression but in the main was one of the most interesting blokes I have ever met, having lived some great times with a full array of stories plotting his cascade through the waterfalls of life and all manner of vaginas.

I sipped my lime and soda (we both had decided to give alcohol a bit of a rest for January) and asked Larry about Lou, his love interest, a sex-driven airhostess who fitted Larry's lust for sex, perfectly well. Sadly, it wasn't clicking or happening the way Larry wanted the relationship to work but Larry had four dates lined up for the week ahead and having seen one candidate already, was planning, in his words, 'to nail the remaining three'. The first one, Larry explained had had the most gorgeous false breasts, which would certainly save her life as a flotation device if the Midlands ever experienced a Tsunami in its canal system. I even got to see some pictures (the modern dating social interaction is impressive—people having their own websites, marketing platform).

I was passed the mobile and briefly scanned the screen, I agreed, nice breasts, "She wouldn't need to float in a flood," I exclaimed, "I'd save her!"

Larry was telling me many of these women on these sites are so hungry for sex, it is a case of meet for a drink, half-way down the first drink after several exchanges of compliments, Larry would start telling them what he would like to do to them in his most polite ex-public school fashion. Incredibly, to my innocent ears, nine times out of ten, they would be straight back to their house, Larry's place or a hotel, knickers down and shagging against the kitchen table or some other rustic piece of furniture. I was amazed—*I have never known that approach work in my limited experience,* I pondered, maybe I was just not forward enough in my day, besides I was married! The range of professions the women he had encountered were from was equally surprising, ballerinas, scientists, photographers, bored house wives, female drummers, colleagues in the profession and neighbours to name but a few. I loved Larry's newest accounts of his escapades each time we met.

For example, Larry had met a call centre helpdesk woman one year and she was very good at her job but like Larry, had a passion for the nightlife. As a part time actress, she would get roles as an extra in films and have the strangest dress sense. I couldn't tell you any film names but to be honest, I doubt you would have heard of them and I doubt she had either! I just imagined most of these films based on what Larry said bordered on the porno, imagining the main actors getting down on it, while, as an extra, Sally drifted into shot offering crisps and nuts!

Sally worked in an office building that Larry visited and it didn't take Larry long to take his opportunity, to explore Sally's lower half between floors when, by chance, they met in the building's lift. In the time it took from the ground floor to the top floor, Larry had practically removed Sally's under garments and startled a secretary waiting to get in the lift when the doors finally opened. Well, if someone on a helpdesk can't help Larry who can…?

After hearing about the women Larry was meeting that week and trying to understand his depression a bit more, he asked me about my forthcoming medical. I hadn't had a company medical for five years, they had once been mandatory but with recessions,

Brexit etc., senior staff now needed to request one. It is, however, all paid up and consists of a full private health care assessment when you do go, which lasts an hour and half. All you have to do as an employee is book it.

I told Larry, I was long overdue the medical and looking forward to asking the quack about a knock I had taken months before, just above my groin with a hockey ball. It still seemed painful with an occasional dull ache apparent from time to time. Good old Larry was concerned and agreed it was a good idea to get it looked at.

"After all," he beamed, "it may impact your sex drive!"

I have always loved the game of hockey, I had played it since the age of 14 and still had the same thrill from the game aged 43. My main club hockey was played at a range of Midlands clubs and I had recently been lucky enough to train with the Wales over 45 squad playing three friendly matches for them against one of my old hockey clubs Worcester, my view being to try and get in the team when at an eligible age 45. If I am honest, I don't think I was good enough to play for Wales but it takes time to come back from injuries and I had had my fair share, having my right knee ACL needing to be rebuilt and the re-stitching of my lip after being hit by a defenders stick. I had been enthusiastic to push myself and give myself a lift after a nasty spate of injuries, I just needed to build more regularity playing club hockey.

I captained a seven-aside team in a summer corporate league for ten weeks every year, which was fast-paced and mixed (men and women). A high standard of players and good fun. My knock, however, had come from a club Veterans game against Worcester. It was a cold evening circa 8 p.m., and the ball had just taken off towards me, I was simply unable to get out of the way as the 60mph missile collided with my body with a loud thud. I remember my mate, Deano (a lifelong pal), asking if I was OK. I replied yes, but it was a strange ache, a cross between one of your testicles landing in your stomach and a permanently dull pain. I battled on but the dull pain was there for weeks on and off. I did, however, concede that men's league hockey is a rough outing and injuries were to be expected week in week out. It was certainly something I wanted to raise with the doctor, especially as I had since psychologically linked the injury to the odd streak of blood in my stools. To me, it didn't seem enough to get the medical profession excited, overall I felt great and assured Larry that I should breeze through my medical.

Larry simply said, "Good man," smiled with his 40 something good looks and started the next instalment of his experience shagging some busty blonde in her Range Rover parked in a layby on a busy road near the motorway. Larry, too, was a risk taker but different risks. He wouldn't hesitate to ask any female he met for a bit of action, give them a lift home and have enough charm and bravado to secure a blowjob en route. According to Larry, it is extremely hard to drive a car while being sucked off, and you need a woman prepared to swallow too!

Pausing his story, he piped up, "By the way, mate, I really hope you get fit nurses and a good looking female doctor, when I had my last medical, they had to wait as I had an erection!"

I had to laugh, "…I will let you know!" I retorted.

Chapter 4
Developing Character

My parents were both bankers, (yes that was a B not a W)..., I was their only child and we lived in the picturesque, quiet but very rural county of Herefordshire.

I recall, as a young boy/early teens, that my parents were social creatures and had an enviable network of friends. I sometimes found myself being looked after by a sitter on weekend evenings (usually some pretty young female graduate/trainee from my dad's bank) and in the summer holidays, long periods of boredom wishing I had a brother, sister or a play companion. I didn't always look forward to the holiday periods, I ended up being looked after by two hippie types while my parents worked. The hippies were a couple, the guy looking like something out of the 60s, with long curly hair and a bushy long beard and his other half long straight hair and sandals (the type that does yoga, was into CND and probably ate magic mushrooms).

They weren't my type at all, they would plan some lengthy cycle ride when they arrived to look after me every day and in all weathers and ensuring I was riding my bicycle in-between them, we would cover miles and miles of Herefordshire countryside daily. Surely, this was some form of child abuse, I considered calling Esther Rantzen's child line and at this rate, I remember thinking, I would be in The Tour De France by the age of 14. The regimented exercise routine was, however, teaching me endurance and stamina, as the French would say Vigeuer! So I took it on myself to get out there and do something about it whenever the hippies didn't have me cycling. I wanted to create some positives and ensure I was having a laugh. Even at an early age, I was in touch with what I was feeling internally and doing something about it.

We were, at the time, living in a modest new-built three-bedroom house on a residential estate in Leominster a small town, in Northern Herefordshire. The estate was still under construction being built out in phases. I would set off on my pushbike dodging diggers and lorries full of rotating cement, or I would be skate boarding down the steepest road on the estate which had been newly tarmacked that I could find. New families would move in each week and I soon found a few like-minded kids (albeit some younger than me), to mess around with on bikes, go-karts, skateboards etc. I was about nine years old at the time.

The estate had lots of building work going on, the builders would down tools promptly at 5 p.m. and leave their part-constructed houses and smouldering fires where they had been burning packaging for building materials, remnant pieces of timber, ready to resume work the next day. At 5:05 p.m., we would make our move and take over the now deserted building site. Whatever the builders had been doing, we resurrected. Sometimes, the next morning, they couldn't understand how the fires had kept going all night, we had, of course, taken the fires to a whole new level burning anything we could lay our hands on and piling it onto the flames, sometimes with dire consequences, a lot of the solvents, sealants left by the builders would initially hiss and literally blow up, sending us running for the trees with a bit of fear but enthusiastic smiles on our faces.

Other kids would come across from a nearby older housing estate and throw stones at us, which we would throw back, dodging their presence in the trees, mud, corridors of the partly built houses, and running up and down scaffolding. These skirmishes became a regular thing after 5 p.m. every night and we needed a strategy, we were coming off worse every time. I took it on myself to lead our merry group and formed the 'Ah oooo gang', 'Ah ooo' being the loud call sign each member had to perfect. Our call sign annoyed the hell out of many people on the estate, mainly adults either out in their gardens or washing their cars, as we hurtled past on our bikes screaming 'Ah ooo' at the top of our voices. It was an odd sound but we had our turf to defend and we knew where each other were, there to assist a stranded gang member.

We had bikes on patrols, look out posts and weapons (mainly different size sticks and throwable stones), this was gangland warfare. We often came off worse in the fights, the kids from the other estate were bigger, rougher and less forgiving. I got thrown down grassy banks a few times, chipped a few teeth from being hit by stones as did my comrades in arms. I like to think we were more intelligent, more refined but they were rough, taller and out to hurt us. On one occasion, I got cornered on my own and thrown by the other gang repeatedly into long stinging nettles. The pain became a numbness after a while, it was more about trying to escape in one piece (a memory I would later remember as an adult drawing comparisons to being thrown into alien processes and needing to survive).

After about ten throws into the long, hairy, stalked plants, I staggered out of the nettles on my knees, saliva and blood around my face, where I had impacted the stones and earth below the foliage, nettle bumps were everywhere. I was only wearing a t-shirt and shorts. While they took a rest before thinking up some other harsh treatment for me, I got my break and ran for my life. I was always a quick runner and managed to stay just ahead until I lost them in the back alleys of the housing estate. My dad did go looking for them but never found them.

On another occasion, I got stopped by these thugs whilst I was out patrolling on my bike and as they surrounded me blocking my route home, they kindly soaked me with bottles of their freshly warm urine. Luckily, their attempts to steel my bike failed, again I picked my moment and escaped the clutches of the rival gang, pedalling away at record speed. I was fast learning a survival instinct and I was toughening up and developing a sense of 'be ready for anything!'

These battles raged on for years, our numbers grew and we had a network of dens, command structure, communication methods and knew our individual tasks to defend our patch, in essence, we had a workable winning strategy. Thinking back, the housing developer, should have retained us as their site security team!

One warm summer day, our gang was all together, we were mucking about in the trees building new dens, when the police stopped us and reported that a clump of masonry forming part of an old chimney stack had been left on the nearby lane, did we

20

know anything about it? A car had unwittingly ploughed into it (clearly not anticipating, a chimney to be in the road).We could see our rival gang a few hundred yards in the distance so were quick to suggest to the police, that they not us, usually caused the trouble on the estate and were the likely culprits. After all, they were older, rougher and on our patch.

The police went straight to them and we heard very little from the rival gang after that. The police never found out one of our gang had actually put the chimney on the road!

The early days of coordinating the Ah ooo gang did, however, instil in me strong organisational skills and in my quest for an always more positive experience in the summer holidays, a love of being around friends. Friends were so important to me then and were to be treasured like family, they helped you through difficult times and were there when the chips were down. I thrived on the positivity vibes I got out of others then and I appreciate that even more today. If there was ever a negative, like being on your own, I would seek to do something about it as soon as I could, for example, work out a fun experience, organise a get together with my pals and feed off the resulting positivity that came from it. I have, of course, applied this so many times since, becoming known as an instigator, organiser and promoter of good times with friends, planned and spontaneous occasions, parties, every meticulous detail covered to ensure maximum positivity. An element of risk, usually high, thrown in for good measure. I was hardly ever down as a result.

My parents were both Welsh from two small communities near Porthcawl, a town in South Wales not far from Swansea. I loved the Welsh connection as a kid (I still do especially with regards to rugby), it just seemed such a friendly culture when I was growing up. Welsh family houses were welcoming places, sometimes with keys left in the door so you could walk right in, always food and drink offered and happy smiley faces. I remember, at my grandparents respective houses, lots of positives sitting around discussing life, eating welsh cakes and lots of singing, many of my older relatives such as grandparents regularly going to choir practice or bursting into hymns sat in their cosy armchairs. I wanted that same feeling from the people around me right through my lifetime, I found people so interesting and they inspired me even at a young age.

I moved around schools quite a bit as a kid which was disruptive for my confidence and I wouldn't say I was ever an academic either, I liked English but struggled to find the interest level in most subjects. I seemed to score very highly on effort though. My parents pushed me towards an education at the nearby private school founded some 300 years ago, but whilst it was fun for a while and there was plenty of sport to keep me motivated and fit, the school went bankrupt while I was there. I, therefore, had yet another school move, aged 12, as a result! This, however, was in the October half-term for me but not for those whom I would be joining at a state school in Hereford, they were back at their studies already.

I was moving from a year of nine pupils, to a state school which had an average year size of 300. I felt a right tool walking into the packed early morning assembly, with every kid suddenly looking at me as the whole assembly paused, I was, of course, wearing a fine tweed jacket and flannel trousers, totally at odds with everyone else. Embarrassed was not the word...it was a massive negative but my natural recourse was to latch onto any positives I could see. Some of the people who offered to show me the ropes, take me under their wing at that time are still close friends today (despite what I did to them on their respective stag dos later in life).

From state school, the natural progression was to sixth form, I was lucky having taken English at O-level a year early, however, my failure to grasp other subjects with the interest levels required, saw me fail to get the necessary grades to be fully accepted. Sixth form required me to re-sit Maths, Biology and Geography GCSEs before they would let me in, I would have to get the grades up to C or above. My pals were taking the mickey out of me at every opportunity and I was truly flying by the seat of my pants in terms of risk, I was very close to the line, getting left behind but I had a positive vibe, gritty determination and effort I could turn on at will. I eventually got accepted to do the three A-levels I had chosen.

I was, however, no more into the A-level subjects than I had been GCSEs and struggled to apply myself, my new interests were drinking and a real fascination for the opposite sex. My lack of interest in subjects was about to change with the mandatory work experience programme run by the careers advisor tutor. On hearing the news about work experience, my mum was keen to suggest I got experience in an industry that would be well paid like law or dentistry. I wasn't so convinced. I had never had a pleasant experience at a dentists and law sounded too much an indoors type of job. I was quite happy watering plants at Do It All, I literally had no interest in any office type role and already felt that I had been steered by my mum to do subjects completely at odds with my interests. This is common with many teenagers, unable to focus at that age with a defined career path and parents are just keen to see their prized sons and daughters secure the best they can. In my view, so far at GCSE level, I had been guided to take on too many subjects beyond my abilities, A-levels I was doing subjects not in line with my interests, I had really followed my mates and what they had chosen.

I suggested to the bohemian looking careers teacher, who sat there in her 60s dress and sandals (I reckoned she drank her own urine), that a spell of work experience at a local law firm would work for me, that would be in line with my mum's expectations at least. I was, however, given the immediate and stark reality check response by Mrs Woodstock, that law was over-subscribed in terms of work experience placements and that I would be struggling to get the grades for law in any event. My mum was quite shocked when I returned home and announced that I would be completing my first professional experience at a local estate agent. My mum was not pleased. It is worth pointing out that Mrs Woodstock was, however, very happy, nobody had yet chosen estate agency for work experience but as my mum pointed out, you really don't need too many qualifications to do estate agency and I would be wasting an opportunity to go onto university to study a specific degree related to a profession.

In actual fact, for me, the opportunity to do Estate Agency was the best thing to happen to me. The positives I soon realised were endless, on my first day, I immediately identified with the relaxed culture, these guys controlled their diaries, could go out of the office as need be, drove around in BMWs and had good lunches. There was the buzz of deals and plenty of people interaction. The one thing that clicked was after I had ended up spending a day on the road with their Chartered Surveyor, I loved every minute of it, valuing houses, driving around towns, villages, looking into the detail of property fabrics, the market and values.

I was finally inspired, inspired to get my arse into gear and want to do this as a profession. I couldn't understand why more sixth formers hadn't opted for property, this was looking like an ideal working environment and after looking into salaries for surveying, I was satisfied I could make this work for me. I engaged the effort machine and started knuckling down to study. Twenty-six years later, I still have a career in the property industry and have had since 1996, living the same positives of the job I identified back then. I still love it! A perfect job and lifestyle choice, so I had ticked the right box workwise, life was going swimmingly well!

Chapter 5
High Jinx, Early Adulthood

My quest for good times, positivity stemmed from my childhood and I loved the spontaneous and the new areas of life's colourful experiences. Some would, perhaps, argue I have no off switch, a poker-faced risk taker, who will take risks right to the edge of a cliff, look over and assess my chances, looking for the positives. A lot of my friends, looking back, have no off switches either, perhaps subconsciously, that is what drew us together. That said, hopefully, most of my friends would look back and agree, those high jinx times in question had been some classic memories, high risk with plenty of alcohol and laughter—it has had positives for me in the working environment too. I always had a good measure of both male and female friends, I loved both and would organise socials which usually spiralled into some manner of high jinx. I surrounded myself with friends who were equally up for a laugh and positive times. I put loads of personal effort into everything I organised, to maximise the positive times that resulted.

At sixth form, my pal, TJ and I ended up doing the same subjects at A-level, one of which was psychology. I think we picked the subject simply as the ratio of women to men was 8:1. Two girls stood out in particular Laura and Sienna, we gradually got talking to them and became good pals as a plutonic four ball. They didn't stay the sixth form psychology course for very long, one ending up a stable hand in the Cotswold, the other moving to Tech College on the campus next door to sixth form, to do secretarial but we stayed close. Sienna had a red Renault 5 which, at the age of 18, was a classy motor, unlike the clapped out vehicles we were using to run around in.

On one occasion, we toured a few Herefordshire countryside pubs in the Renault, Sienna driving (the sober one for the evening), TJ and I in the back seat, the girls in the front seats. As lads do, when you are not the driver for the evening, we set about necking a few fine ales at each pit stop, we would be at a pub for 45 minutes then onto the next one, more excitement developing as we absorbed more and more of the amber nectar the evening progressing, darkness falling about us. As we looked forward to our next pub, the Renault speeding along under Sienna's control, TJ and I had a brief conversation in whispers in the shrouded blackness of the rear seating area. It was time to expand our level of friendship and trust. Full of bravado, whilst on the way to one pub, and after agreeing a pact based on our newfound trust, we wound down our respective rear windows.

I remember our agreed plan through the shadowy veil of alcohol, as, simultaneously, we grabbed the handle located above each of our respective passenger back doors and crawled slowly out into the buffeting, windy night air. As we wriggled keeping hands firmly on the handles, we were placing our bottoms on the door itself where the windows had been, each on different sides of the car. Gradually, we moved our free arm over the roof and grasped each other's free arm, smiling at the relief of connecting bodies. The scary bit was letting go of the handle inside the car and then linking both arms over the roof, most of our bodies were then more out of the car as opposed to inside. What a great positive feeling it was being in the rushing night air with someone you trusted experiencing the same thing, effectively each other's lives literally in each other's hands.

By the time Laura and Sienna realised what was happening, TJ and I were shouting faster, faster and on the straight roman road past the Hereford racecourse, Sienna hit 70mph on the Renault 5's speedometer. What a rush but we trusted each other implicitly and I felt safe, I would not die. I remembered that feeling and would use the same inner belief to confront risk later in life. We had to get back in the vehicle which was harder in many ways but we perfected reversing the process, gradually lowering ourselves carefully back into the vehicle, hair majorly out of place but our new game had been a real blast, living on the edge, knowing the risk and dicing with it.

The risk taking went on, we became bolder, confident in our survival. A few months after the roof top activities, TJ and I were again in the back of another student's car, Jake. Jake was a sporty guy into his weight lifting but he didn't strike me as a confident driver but he was, at the time, my future wife, Claudia's best friend. On this particular evening, we were just along for the ride cruising some different village pubs, to TJ and I, it was simply an opportunity for us both to drink more beer with a chauffeur and female company too. After last orders, we headed back towards Hereford down some obscure country lanes. TJ and I were again in the back, Claudia and Jake in the front. Again, in the dark excitement of the back seat, the occasional street light illuminating our faces for brief seconds at a time, we had our quick whispered discussion and then, without warning, proceeded to get the well-rehearsed plan into effect, getting the back windows of the MG Maestro down and getting out onto the roof linking arms in the cool night air.

"Faster, faster," we shouted and much to Claudia's shock, Jake truly obliged by accelerating the car as best he could. (Maybe he was trying to impress Claudia or us with his rallying skills but for us, this was now a lot harder on narrow twisty lanes, with every turn and increased G Force, it was becoming harder to hold on to each other and there was no opportunity to wriggle back into the vehicle.) We managed to shout our shared concerns about his driving at each other over the roof and tightened our grip.

I was shouting loudly through the buffeting night air, "Hold on, buddy, 90 degree bend coming…" then it was like slow motion, we saw the accident happening. The car locked its wheels screeching loudly on the downhill straight leading to the bend, a bend Jake was never going to make with all the rubber in the world, his car sliding quickly towards the bend…

"…Brace," shouted TJ, an eager nervousness in his voice, as the car left the road and went nose first into the ditch which lay between the edge of the road and mountainous hedge. The back of the car flew up in the air, as our respective hips and legs collided with the top of the doorframe, I felt the pain of the collision on my pelvis. The engine was still revving, it was noisy and there was a smell of burnt rubber, exhaust fumes, manure…but here we were, still linked arms in unison over the roof…regardless of anything else, we breathed through the pain and with relieved smiles which turned into laughter, celebrated being alive and having been lucky not to fly over the 10ft hedge in front of the bonnet. Claudia and Jake were in shock, blaming me for instigating a dangerous prank and risking all our lives.

Personally, it was Jake's speed into the bend that was to blame but as we clambered out, we appreciated how lucky we had been. The back end of the Maestro was 6ft up in the air and we had to jump out to the ground. It took all four of us to get the car down as it pivoted on the edge of the ditch. TJ and I laughed and laughed, high-adrenalin funnelling through our bodies, living the risk. There was not a scratch on Jake's car, until we were pushing the front of the car away from the ditch and TJ accidentally pushed his front headlight in, we didn't tell him.

It was though we were both dicing with death, we were, however, confident in our abilities in confronting risk.

These were irresponsible actions but done for the crack, we knew the risks but didn't seem to care. Life was simply what it was, perhaps we just didn't appreciate its full value yet, unbeknown to me, how I would come to value life in later years.

We were completely reckless, at 18 years old, TJ would pick me up in his dad's 2.0i Sierra and we would cruise the city roads and narrow lanes. On one chilly night, we drove into the public car park at a nearby woodland beauty spot, with all the Sierra's lights off after spotting the chalky blue Mark 1 Fiesta of a fellow male student now bonking an ex-girlfriend of mine, Katrina. They didn't see or hear our approach as the Sierra crept across the car park, TJ rolling the car to 5 foot from the Fiesta's passenger door. You could just make out the naked torsos through the steamed up windows, the Fiesta gently rocking from side to side as I imagined Katrina taking the leading role in the vehicle. I remember thinking…she never brought me to this place, not to bonk anyway!

Perhaps this was the birth place of dogging but I didn't have time to think any more about it, TJ hit all the Sierra's lights shouting, "Yeeha, mother fuckers…" lighted fog lights, head lights were now on full beam as at that moment a pair of naked tits hit the steamed up window, an arm covering Katrina's eyes through blindness like a startled rabbit caught in the confusion of sudden blinding light.

TJ hit reverse, sending the Sierra rapidly backwards, executing an impressive hand break turn as we then were moving forwards speeding quickly back onto the main road. We laughed and laughed and loved the positive, feeling the risk. We laughed even more when the scared occupants of the Fiesta over took us on the route back to Hereford oblivious to our vehicle being the cause of illuminating their romantic moment courtesy of Ford motors. I wondered whether they would opt for such a public place next time. It wasn't long after that time, Katrina left the country.

Chapter 6
The Hospital Medical, February 2016

The company I worked for going back 20 years or so, would request senior employees must attend an annual medical in a private medical practice in London. It was mandatory and when I joined in 2000, it was a bit of a secret joke for existing employees and the way it was sold to new starters like me. I remember my boss, Charles, at the time saying, "You have your medical next week, don't you? Remember to keep your knees up!" The comment confused me and was lost on me, surely, he must of meant, keep your chin up! Charles had simply smiled at the time and walked off.

The medical was just off Harley Street, a small discreet surgery clinic, I was greeted from the waiting room by a Dr Gelardo, an elderly plump man looking like Captain Chaos off The Cannon Ball Run. We talked for a while in his treatment room after which he told me to strip and started taking a keener interest in my tackle and naked anatomy. The medical was taking ages and his equipment and methods to me seemed really primitive, with painful metal type ECG disks with old looking wires, leaving red saucer shaped welts on the skin after removal.

It was then I heard the phrase, "Now, please lie on your side and put your knees up near your chin!" I pondered for a split second the similarity of this statement to my manager Charles' comments the previous week but before I had time to contemplate further thoughts on the matter, I raised my knees upwards towards my chin as instructed. Suddenly, there was an impact as Dr Gelardo's finger bounced off my arsehole. What the fuck just happened? I thought in sudden shock. I desperately tried to work out this new invasive experience to one of my most sensitive areas. While these thoughts raced through my mind, Dr Gelardo told me to relax as he moved in for a second go. Given I had received no real warning of the prostate check other than

30

the phrase 'knees to your chin', I endured the unexpected violation and then it dawned on me, I now completely understood the joke and other comments from blokes in the office that I hadn't understood at the time. I walked away from Dr Gelardo surgery, walking like John Wayne with a gaited stagger, feeling humiliated. It took me a day or so to get this straight in my mind and duly joined in the banter when I was back in the office with the next new employee getting ready for their medical.

Now, it was my turn to have fun, asking, "What has its head between its knees and a hand sticking out of its arse…tell me the answer next week…?"

The company medicals eventually migrated to a national private health care company, I am sure Dr Gelardo wasn't most people's first choice, the health care company package offered more benefits, giving more flexibility on location of the medical as opposed to individuals trekking down to Harley Street and another bonus was that the finger up the arsehole prostate check, was only necessary after certain age levels. Gelardo, in my view, was doing arsehole examinations for the hell of it, I didn't need a prostate check in my view, I seriously thought I am too young to be in danger of this type of disease and too fit and healthy for cancer to get me.

Following the recession, medicals were no longer mandatory in our firm and became available on an employee's request only, albeit costs were still covered by the company. I slipped conveniently into a pattern of no medicals, I was, after all, feeling great on the most part.

In January 2016, I realised my last medical had been as far back as five years ago. Time had simply flown by, I was, however, intrigued to know if I was in better shape than last time, I wondered whether my BMI had come down, cholesterol lowered and would they think my hockey ball incident was something to worry about. I, therefore, booked a medical with a health insurance company in January 2016.

The morning of the medical, I had abstained, as directed, from food in order that the blood tests would be as accurate as possible. First off, I was shown into see the nurse (two nurses in fact), neither of which I concluded would impress Larry. Well saying that they didn't impress me in the looks department either,

Larry might have been more forgiving. They took my vital signs: weight, height, bloods, blood pressure etc. and had me doing a mini work out on the floor, while they sat quietly on chairs watching and taking notes. I did wonder if this was a wind up, me on the floor doing the most pathetic work out possible with two nurses gazing on silently. I did, however, now understand why I had been told that I needed to pack shorts and a t-shirt for the procedure. The work out wasn't hard but apparently, a large degree of the UK population simply can't pass this simple workout test. I was shocked and was keen to show my ability, impressing the nurse and her trainee with my press-ups, squat thrusts and sit-ups. At least I think they were impressed?

After finishing my mini-fitness session with the nurses, I was shown into see the doctor, she was female but built like a cross between Dawn French and Johnny Vegas with too much makeup on. Friendly though and clearly knowledgeable and it was obvious to me she totally knew her stuff. I was thinking Larry would be disappointed with my report back on the nurses and doctor but who cared, so far I was flying this medical. I felt good.

I remember the doctor comparing the medical I had just endured with the one I had completed five years ago and congratulating me on keeping within my BMI and parameters for my age. There were no concerns on bloods etc. and I had, as I knew, passed my mini-workout. It appeared I was in good shape.

At this point in the medical, it was more of a chat, the facts and figures out of the way and we delved into my mental shape and stability. We both concluded (nothing to worry about there) and I was then asked "Is there anything else concerning you?" It is the type of question men can easily say, '…no, I am fine, nothing more to add, doc!' and with doctors, you get so little time to make that call on whether you want to discuss anything at that point in time.

"Yes, actually, I am a bit worried about some bleeding I have had in my stools and it might be related to a hockey ball impact…" there we are, I had said it. No turning back now and I genuinely thought, at that time, I would be wasting another doctor's time.

I had gone against my better judgment and now knew that there was a strong chance that the female Johnny Vegas would be taking a closer look. I could have walked out of this joint, with a clean bill of health, what was I doing?

Before I knew it, she was asking me when, how much bleeding…my answer being not much and infrequently, the type of blood etc. it isn't an easy thing for you reading this chapter to read about, I am sure but harder to talk about to a sizeable woman with an intent in her eye to shove her finger up your arse!

Without further hesitation, the doctor rose to her feet, washed her hands in the sink and said, "I'd better check your prostate!"

…Well, at least she asked, Dr Gelardo could have immediately learnt something from her, simply saying knees to your chin was not her approach and I felt slightly more comfortable. Furthermore, Larry would find this episode of my medical interesting. With the snap of latex gloves against her wrists, in she went…

"I can't see anything, Mr Beavan!"

I bit my tongue wanting to respond, "I have a torch in the car if you need it!"

"All I can say is that if you want to know where the blood is coming from, it must be coming from further up, you would need further camera investigation, a simple procedure. I can report this to your GP and suggest you might look into this but it is really up to you."

I said my goodbye to Miss Vegas—feeling slightly closer to her than before and thinking I should have asked for a picture for Larry's benefit but ultimately I left that medical feeling I had passed and there wasn't really anything to worry about, it had all been positive with just one more test if I opted for it. I was inclined not to bother.

As a bloke, I really felt like I was wasting the medical professions time especially if I was to go through with more tests only to be given the all clear. I compared myself to others my age and thought, surely they won't be wasting time with pointless tests. I needed to think, mull this over, I didn't feel I needed to rush this.

Sure enough, Miss Vegas wrote to my GP giving them a copy of my medical and the all clear but mentioning my bleeding and that a further test would be the only opportunity to know for sure the cause or if it pointed to something more serious. I received a copy of the same report, part of me thought I would get a call from my GP proactively suggesting I take up the test but GPs simply don't work like that anymore, not in my experience anyway. This would be down to me to get my arse into gear or not, (excuse the pun)...meanwhile, time passed.

Engaging the part of my brain that said 'you should get this test done' took time, I admit, you need to adapt your mind-set that while everything feels normal and routine in life, there could be something serious going on that could change all of that. Health ultimately needs to be taken seriously and whether you lead the process or the medical professionals drive it, it should be embraced.

Chapter 7
Deep Water, 1990–1993

Despite my risk taking, disregard for life, there were a number of skills for life that I was still developing, I was a young adult in 1990, 18 years old loving my independence. I was an organiser of anything fun, a lover of being with friends and striving for the positive but there was still that undefinable undertone of risk and high jinx, dicing with death. One night, we had taken TJ's dad's car to a house party on a farm out in 'the sticks', a village, 10 miles or so west of Hereford. A nice friend of ours from Sixth Form, had, unwittingly, suggested a party while his parents were abroad and foolishly invited TJ, myself and some other friends. These type of parties were the best, all manner of things to get up to and space, no parental controls.

In the car, on the way, I was thinking…I had my eye on taking a combine harvester for a spin if I could find one with keys in it and somewhere to put my beer. There were four of us in the car, Chloe my best female friend in the front, Fred… (Who incidentally is now her hubby) in the back with me. It was raining hard travelling there in TJ's dad's Ford Sierra and as we turned for the farm, driving along the narrow hedge-lined lane to the farm, we crossed a narrow stream. That part of the lane was a ford, the lane literally disappeared into the water and re-emerged on the other side of the stream. It wasn't deep but crossing it was the only means of getting to the farmhouse. The party was a good one and six hours later when we said our goodbyes and had checked that all farm equipment was back in its correct location, we retraced our route back down the farm track, it was tipping it down, it was still raining hard.

The water level of the ford was, however, a lot higher, there were no sides to the stream any longer and it was in flood, flowing fast. TJ, ever confident, decided it was doable if we kept the car in first gear, half-clutch, high revs keeping the water blown out of the exhaust. (Later in my life, I was part of a voluntary river rescue, mountain rescue and swift water rescue organisation, a blue lights charity on call to the police, fire brigade, ambulance service and RAF), knowing now what I didn't know then, proceeding by car into the ford in flood was a reckless, a life-threatening decision. It was such a dangerous move, high-risk is an understatement and there would have been no one to rescue us.

Halfway across the ford, the water came over the bonnet and in through the doors filling the foot wells, our shoes now submerged. The noise of the water crashing against my passenger door was deafening, an angry watercourse, the flow of water trying to deal with the unexpected vehicle now blocking its least path of resistance. The car swayed as if it would lift up and at one point, we stopped and it sounded like the engine would die, as TJ desperately increased the revs. Despite seemingly impossible odds and all by this time petrified, we somehow managed to get to the other side but the car was fucked.

We spent the next hour laughing about how lucky we were to still be alive but whilst we celebrated that fact we were emptying the foot wells with our shoes, which we used as water carrying vessels. The real damage was in the engine, the car no longer fired on four cylinders, it was now a shadow of its former self, the Sierra now operating on only 2 cylinders which provided limited horsepower, as we limped back to Hereford at 20mph top speed, everything soggy.

TJ's dad didn't take it well, I remember him standing there in his pyjamas saying, "Oh TJ, oh TJ…what have you done to my car?" The car had to be stripped back to shell…but look at the positives, it was a laugh of sorts and it was a truly great feeling that we had survived, another close shave. A few weeks later, the car was written off in any event as TJ, myself and his new girlfriend were in a fairly nasty smash on a major junction near the river bridge, hit side on by an army guy and his pregnant wife as we lacked enough road awareness and distracted, turned across their path, it being their right of way, our fault completely.

In that moment of the crash, I had to help TJ's girlfriend out over the front seats as the smell of fuel was all around us. She was in tears, bless her, panicking as her door was now misshapen and unusable. Cars driving in both directions towards that part of the road couldn't see the tail lights of either crashed vehicle, as the vehicles were at angles. As a result, lots of cars needed to swerve, skidding violently to avoid the crash, petrol and oil on the road. Again, we smiled when we got out, we celebrated that we were alive.

Despite the scrapes I was getting myself into, I had a thirst for more and I was a survivor, I wanted more. It wasn't that long after the Anaglypta roll incident, that I planned a road trip with Digger from Hereford to Brecon inviting a few of the guys from Do It All and a few from Sixth Form. The plan was to leave one Saturday evening after work and drive while it was light. Digger's father had an estate with an eight-acre lake and two-storey boathouse, it was our intention to stay there overnight.

At the time, one of our group had managed to accumulate several yellow flashing lights from the top of JCB diggers, these were easily obtainable by cutting the wire leading to the light and pulling the light, with its magnetic base, off the top of the digger cab. A simple device could then be attached to the end of the wire, enabling it to act as your very own flashing emergency vehicle light when plugged into your car cigarette lighter. We handed out five or six of these lights to each vehicle in our convoy and set off for the dizzy heights of the Welsh mountains.

I think it was on the Brecon dual carriageway which was heavily traffic-coned due to road works, that both Digger and I in our respective cars, donned our flashing emergency lights and drove into the access only traffic-coned section of the dual carriageway. Even in those days, there was little sign of activity by the Highways Authority, they had downed tools for the evening. The rest of our convoy followed suit and attached their flashing emergency lights following the lead cars onto the wrong side of the traffic cones. All the holidaymakers, camper vans and OAPs thought this was bizarre, I am sure but in the confusion, followed the convoy. It was now difficult for anyone following us to understand which side of the traffic cones we should be on. For about a mile, we carried on, driving on the works repair section of the dual carriageway, until the reason for the cones having been there in the first place, became apparent…a huge hole in that section of the road. Knocking over several cones in the process, Digger's MGB Roadster and my Mk 1 fiesta 1.1, burst back onto the correct side of the traffic cones and carriageway. In our mirrors, there was carnage, traffic cones flying up in the air, cars and vans making sharp turns on spotting the hole rapidly appearing before their eyes. Needless to say, we quickly unplugged our emergency lights, took them off our car roofs and left the chaos behind us, laughing endlessly from the buzz of what had just happened. We were reckless idiots but learning skills and pushing the limits.

The party that followed was a typical spontaneous catalogue of memorable events. We took over the small two-storey boathouse next to the lake and proceeded to get very drunk. I recall one of the lads being pushed out onto the water in a rowing boat with only one oar. The other one got burnt on the fire keeping us warm (there was no heating). All of this, while one of the guests hammered out tunes on an old piano, a number of guests trapped upstairs as the door had broken at the bottom of the staircase. The next morning, the guy in the boat with one oar, was now in the middle of the lake, hoarse from shouting to be rescued and dizzy from going around in circles. I remember him waving at me through the early morning mist clinging to the water, I simply waved back.

As times moved on, Do It All became a distant memory, the majority of my group of friends progressing to various universities. In my case, my grades weren't quite as expected, so I ended up on a slightly different course to that intended but destined for the same outcome, I was on my way to Bristol Polytechnic. Interestingly, Digger decided not to go to university but instead, signed up to Marks and Spencers' management training programme. I suspect it was the free Y-fronts which attracted him but either way, he would still turn up at my university digs on a weekend with much needed cigarettes and beer money and with a set of wheels.

We would sit around chain smoking Dunhill or Marlborough Lights and drinking cans of Fosters until we came up with an idea for entertainment. This usually involved literally gathering a few pals together and heading off in various cars to a house party in say, London where we knew someone.

I would usually end up on the parcel shelf of the MGB Roadster, quite happy smoking a fag and drinking a can of larger, the throaty growl of the bored out MG engine echoing off the terraced houses as we meandered through the streets of Bristol to the motorway.

One such party, we were midway down the M4, in a VW Passatt, on a road trip when someone produced a huge rolly, a spliff… apparently, which was new to me. It was a big spliff and all four of us in the car partook filling the car with smoke. I remember laughing so much and not really noticing the drive to London. The party itself was at my friend, Chloe's house which she shared with four other girls in Roehampton.

One of the girls was from a family that rented accommodation to Premiership footballers new to their football club and apparently, a few were scheduled to come to the house party. I knew nothing about football but was completely stoned on arrival and for most of the party. I tried walking along the top of a garden fence at one point which collapsed under me. Again, I found this hilarious. The footballers did turn up, I didn't have a clue who they were but they all sounded very Italian to me. They agreed to listen to a song my roommate and I had written about a fellow student who had had his front grill stolen from the front of his car. The song was called: *'Lunty, where has your grill gone?'* We were so stoned, giggling, trying to sing the song, me on a harmonica and singing intermittently and my friend on his acoustic guitar.

At this point, you're thinking that doesn't sound like a classic song and you would be perfectly correct in that assumption, especially when sung by two stoned students. The footballers could have spent the night in a top London club and after the first verse, were probably wishing they had, instead they quietly left us singing in the garden, locked the patio doors from the inside and put on Madonna full volume. We didn't care if the famous Italian footballers of this world didn't embrace popular student folk songs and we had a great time, we kept up our singing in the garden annoying the neighbours.

Some weekends and in the holidays, I would travel back to Hereford where the good times continued. A large group of pals back from their respective universities would meet up with the likes of TJ, Digger and I and climb Hay Bluff, one of the famous slopes of the Black mountains. We would take a sand sledge and sledge down the steep grass. At the bottom, we would attach a long rope to the back of Digger's car, taking it in turns to be towed across the grassy plateau at the bottom of Hay Bluff, seeing who would fall off with the best tumble through the corners. The wipeouts were painful, keeping your cigarette in one piece was really tough but necessary as a student on little money. Bewildered couples out for a quiet drive up the mountain, now sat in their parked cars with half-eaten sandwiches, their view spoilt by students on sledges careering around in front of them. We didn't care, we were having great times, positive spontaneous fun, with plenty of risk…right on the edge but we were in control.

On another return trip from university back to Hereford, I met with Digger and TJ for a round of golf at Hereford racecourse, there was an 18-hole municipal course in the middle of the racecourse. I was completely shit at golf and wasn't that keen but it was a municipal course and how hard could it be? I think it was about hole three where we met some other pals by chance and ended up playing six players to one hole as opposed to our previous three.

It was confusing for me not being as fluent as the others with my swing and working out whose go it was. On hole six, I opened up my swing and hit a lovely lofty ball but gauging where it was going to land I felt that stomach churning sickness as I had when the roll of Anaglypta had almost killed Digger. I had spotted TJ marching in strides towards his bunkered ball, clubs on his back right near to where I thought my golf ball would land. TJ was directly in the flight path. I think you are meant to shout 'Four' but in the haste of onset panic, I shouted 'Duck'. TJ may have looked up momentarily searching for a duck in flight but in that same moment, the topflight ball hit him smack on the back of his head, the force of the ball sending him into a kind of somersault into the bunker below.

For the second time in my life the person stood next to me, this time Digger said, "I think you have killed him!" and we duly rushed over to find TJ lying unmoving on his back in the bunker, blood soaking the sand.

Luckily, he moved his arm pulled out a Marlborough, lit it and still lying there said, "Which one of you fuckers was it?"

…He was of course looking at me.

I confessed and we promptly took TJ to A&E. Even today, he still has a bald patch on the back of his head where he got hit.

I was making a habit out of hitting people on their heads with objects but both, so far, had survived.

Chapter 8
The Dance of the Flaming Arseholes, May 2002

One of the first opportunities for Digger to get me back for the Anaglypta incident came on my stag do in 2002. I was 32.

I had left the planning of my stag do to my best men, one of which was coming from Sydney especially, the other now an officer in the army (TJ). The organiser I am, I had to get involved, however, with the basic structure, organising a two night stag do tour to include clubbing Friday night with a welsh male voice choir thrown in by my father en route. Saturday, I had planned for the 17 of us to play hockey against the local Hockey Club team I played for at the time, to then all jump on a minibus or charabanc to Wales, back to my ancestral home Porthcawl.

The bit of my stag do which I didn't plan was the challenge element organised by my best man. The idea was simple, keep the groom on the edge of drunkenness while everyone would arrive pre-armed with a challenge, which I would have to complete during the course of the weekend. The challenges ranged from Irish Tequila slammers where you snort salt and squeeze lemon in your eyes, you still drink the tequila. Then there were the dares testing out chat up lines to random women dressed in a peculiar outfit, 'Your eyes are like spanners, when you look at me my nuts tighten!'

...I remember the look on the poor welsh girl's face, 'A spanner she said?' These were the easier ones, the challenges got progressively worse. I was unexpectedly rugby tackled on opening my hotel room door by several of my stag do mates and promptly tarred and feathered in my hotel room after enduring a ferocious struggle until my energy was sapped by the weight of burly masculine types each holding a limb or leaning against me. Tarred and feathered basically means I was stripped naked and covered with black boot polish, feathers from the pillows which they had split open and white flour.

When they departed, I lay there, still for a moment, as a feather drifted slowly downwards past the end of my nose and landing on the bedside table. I was shocked by the state of the room and when I eventually clambered to my feet, it looked like a chicken had had a fight with an oil well and Windy Miller's barn. The duvet, walls etc. were covered with a mix of black streaks of boot polish and the contrasting white feathers and flour. I was now panicking, imagining the life ban from the hotel chain I was about to experience due to the state of my room, my actions as a guest unexplainable. I then went into the en suite and was scrubbing frantically in the shower and sink but only seemingly exporting the black polish to the white ceramic of the bathroom fittings. However, even this small episode on the stag do was nothing compared to Digger's challenge and I didn't see it coming, I felt it first!

The minibus, late on the Saturday afternoon, had reached Wales and in a small village, on the outskirts of Porthcawl, where we found a good friendly pub. A local band was knocking out great tunes and there was a fantastic atmosphere, so we decided to stay for a few rounds of beer. The pub had a small, walled beer garden and we were drinking heavily, all dressed in the same polo shirt tour tops with a red dragon logo and Beavans Dragons embroidered above, each stag do member then had a personalised number and nickname embroidered on their top.

I was getting used to challenges being read out by this time and after being tarred and feathered, I was of the mind-set, I was literally prepared for anything, a skill I can recommend for life. However, it was Digger's challenge, and whilst this one started OK, as it was read out by one of my best men, it soon deteriorated.

"Stand on one of the picnic tables," initially, as TJ paused reading his challenge, I thought, *Is that it!* It will take more than that to embarrass me! I smiled to myself another challenge down, how simple, I've succeeded, I am not embarrassed in front of the various couples out for a quiet drink, discussing their futures and weekends but then, without warning, Digger joined me on the table.

"I need to demonstrate this one to you first," he said smiling. With that, he dropped his trousers and pants and got handed a full pint. This was all pre-planned. Then someone handed him ten sheets of toilet paper. Digger explained that one end of the ten sheets went up your arse held between your cheeks, the other floated gently in the wind. The idea was to down your pint but only once someone had lit the free end of the toilet paper chain. At this point, the rest of the stag do were now gathered closely around the table, there was little that the rest of the pub guests could see apart from a large group of men standing around a table laughing.

Someone lit the free end of toilet paper and I was amazed by the ferocity and speed of the flames moving quickly towards his bottom but Digger managed to down his drink just in time, hauling his trousers up and pulling the paper away from his rear. With that, he smiled and said, "Your turn!" to rapturous applause.

It would be embarrassing enough downing your trousers and pants in front of all your mates and the other drinkers in the pub garden, let alone shoving one end of toilet paper up your arse but now, my mates were goading all pub dwellers to watch the free novelty act. In these scenarios, they are unexpected but it is about adapting your mind to a situation, however odd it may seem at the time and about making a decision quickly.

Someone once told me it is better to make a decision even if the wrong one, than to be indecisive. Look for the positives in everything, even if, with a situation like this, they are hard to identify. I got handed a full pint and prepared myself as I was told to shove the free end of toilet paper up my bottom. I remember the audience, now some 100 or so people cheering and shouting things like, "What if he sets fire to the picnic table, or worse, the pub, I only have 20 pounds in my wallet!"

As I was saying the words, "Tell me when it is lit…?" I had the initiative to have my pint glass ready at my lips…it was then someone shouted, "We lit it already!"

Someone else shouted, "There's six sheets, not ten, get drinking!" I suddenly felt the heat of fire on my arse cheeks…my instinct told me to drink, which I did with gusto until the pain of burning flesh kicked in, my arse was literally being burnt and my arsehole. I turned quickly in horror to witness a glow of bright flames all around my rear quarters, whilst the laughter and cheers were deafening. I used the remainder of the pint to douse the flames, a really tricky manoeuver while stood on a picnic bench trying to put out a fire you can't completely see, your trousers around your ankles. I need not have feared for becoming a 999 call in Wales that evening, another few pints were thrown over me by my knowledgeable mates at what they perceived as a human candle or the early stages of spontaneous human combustion. I turned from a walking inferno to almost needing a snorkel. Everyone was pissing themselves laughing as Digger said, "Well done, mate...!" 'The dance of the flaming arseholes!'

Apparently, the frantic moves I made along with the yelps and cries, made me look like a dad dancing. I would never forget this moment, the throbbing pain inflicted on such a personal area...still, I couldn't complain too much...I had nearly killed Digger with a roll of Anaglypta! This was payback.

As much as I couldn't walk after the incident, not to mention the soggy underpants and blistered arse cheeks, I loved my mates, I drew so much from people around me, even ones who enjoyed watching your bum being seriously on fire. I took the positive that they respected me a bit more for doing it and that I was game for a laugh. When I needed them for real, they would support me.

I remember the last stag do challenge called 'Bright Eyes'...I was stood at the end of the evening in the foyer of the hotel we were booked into on the outskirts of town, when the challenge was read out. I had to walk around the hotel foyer with my tackle in a pint glass of ice cubes singing *'Bright eyes burning like fire, bright eyes...'*

I was very drunk, and I think the receptionist had seen worse during the course of her employment and the way I saw things, at least I wasn't on fire, so this was bliss in comparison. My knob was blue though at the end of the challenge and what was left was throbbing with cold, but I was surviving and at least my mates were having a good laugh at my expense.

There were some heavy hangovers on the Sunday, as we travelled on the minibus back to Hereford. It was about half way back to Hereford that the minibus, driven by my mate Duncan, veered off the main Brecon road back to Hereford and diverted down a single track lane signposted Langorse Lake. We were near Brecon and I was told we were just stopping for people to use facilities and ultimately, we would be stretching our legs. Everybody was out of the minibus quickly and taking in the air down by the lake edge. It was then I realised there was an air of anticipation, an atmosphere of prior planning, they were going to take me down.

I ran at the assembled mass and landed a few punches, knees in the groin before the 16 somewhat shocked group re-assembled some order and over-powered me, stripping me naked for the third time that weekend and left me tied to a bench next to the water's edge draped in a welsh flag and with an inflatable kangaroo strapped above. It was then the defining moment came, with lots of laughter and shouts, they were gone, gone back to Hereford some 30 miles away leaving me to silence, apart from the gentle lapping of the water and occasional quack from a passing duck.

An old lady who happened to be feeding the ducks just looked at me. Initially, I wondered if she had some long lost desire to abuse a man of my age, with some warped sexual tension but I was still drunk and I, therefore, nervously asked her to help me. The lady continued to stare, an almost palatable evident loathing seeping from her eyes despising every man she had ever met, she tossed another piece of bread at the gathering ducks and just carried on staring, perhaps punishing me for that one man in her life who refused to take her virginity. I concluded I was on my own, as I wriggled under my bindings to try and get free.

With no assistance from her, I managed to free myself after a good 20 minutes and wrapped in the only thing I had, the welsh flag and taking Skippy the kangaroo along with me for company, I went to the local shop nearby. Nobody is that helpful, I found, if you don't have money or you are half-naked. I think, they assume you have been on magic mushrooms in that part of the world.

After some negotiation to use a phone, a taxi eventually came, but as I had no means of making payment, the driver would only take me back to their office in Brecon first, before agreeing to eventually take me home to Hereford. I remonstrated that my arse had been truly set on fire, but it's difficult explaining that to a taxi driver who thinks you might be a mental patient.

"Smell the air," I said, "I can still smell burnt flesh!"

...He didn't say a word.

It took hours to get back to Hereford...and there they all were, my loyal friends, waiting in my parents' garden until they had sanctity of knowledge that I had safely arrived, clearly through morbid curiosity but in the main, glad to see me home.

Chapter 9
Everything Is Perfect...for a While

Larry was, thankfully, relaxed, sat opposite me in our usual spot in the comfy leather seats in the corner of the bar lounge area. I could tell he was pleased with his latest female meeting with tinder's latest offering, having got off first base without having to wine and dine the lady for more than what seemed to be two hours.

"She likes chocolate bars too!" he exclaimed, "She's a Crunchie girl, a big fan like me!" I needed to pause for breath, my imaginative mind struggled to get this particular vision out of my brain, the idea of Larry turning up to a first date with his left over Christmas selection box and suggesting these sweet treats had far more potential as sex aids provided they had been kept in the fridge all morning.

As Larry spoke, my mind drifted, I thought back to the recent medical and my own recent prostate examination by Dr Vegas, trying to understand why anyone would want to shove a Crunchie up their arse for sexual gratification.

"So what was the nurse like, did you get a female doctor?" enquired the interested Larry.

I explained to Larry that there wasn't much to report and that I had pretty much been given an all clear by Dr Vegas and had been given a more thorough examination of my back passage than a Twirl or Crunchie would ever achieve.

I added, "I may, however, need a closer look further up, a telescopic thing in an operation, it's up to me."

After some discussion, I agreed with Larry that I would think it over, again, I was conscious about wasting the medical profession's time and it didn't feel like a major decision that would, for example, impact my ultimate survival. I thought back to occasions where I had needed to make decisions or take responsibility, there was no rush here surely, other than a few hockey knocks, I felt fine. Larry was keen to take my place if I decided not to pursue the procedure, for him, this was a new potential sexual experience.

In 2009, I had found myself really bored and needed a form of escapism from the work environment, call it a midlife crisis if you like but I wanted to do something akin to my mates with their physical jobs, I was envious. TJ, who had coaxed me down from the racking in the Anaglypta incident, was now one of Britain's leading bomb disposal experts and risking his life for Queen and Country regularly. I often wish I had joined the army and really wanted something much more than a desk job.

I found myself drawn to any news relating to lifeboats and search and rescue and by chance found myself at King George the Fifth playing fields in Hereford where there was a typical summer show on, with various stands dotted around the playing fields. One of these stands was a search and rescue organisation and they were there with an orange and black 6 metre rib, all kitted out with blue lights and all the rescue gear and a tooled up Land rover Defender, with its winch and emergency blue lights integrated into the grill and on the roof plus rescue sledges on the roof. I met a lovely lady who was their executive secretary or similar and she pointed to the fact that they were looking for members, but it would be useful if I could bring something to the party in the form of skill sets. Being fit and active wasn't quite enough and after a discussion, it appeared I didn't have the right skills currently.

It was a very well respected charity dispatched by the Police, Ambulance service, RAF and Fire Brigade to assist in river, estuary, sea and land /mountain search and swift water rescue. The charity covered inland waterways with four search and rescue stations, one located on the Severn Estuary, a section of water with the second highest tide in the world, at its highest approximately 60ft.

As I drove home, I concluded, I very much wanted this voluntary role in my life and set about researching the skills I would need. I ended up signing up and doing my RYA Power Boating course in Bristol and my advanced driving (Master driver) in my spare time and at my own cost. It was all about pushing myself, even though I was busy enough with a young family and role running a department at work. I joined their

Worcestershire station on a probation and soon was swamped with new things to learn, techniques for search and rescue, handling speedboats in serious floodwater, VHF radio skills, knots and first aid. There was plenty of driving rescue vehicles, helming rescue boats and outdoor life, it was hard work after the day job but I loved it. Within time, I became an operational crewmember on call, on a pager and also progressed rapidly to sit on the executive board of the charity. The charity had 150 members and I hoped I could bring my business skill set to the role. It was hard and again, a lot of work as a volunteer, the charity had no paid roles either so what you got out of it was a different set of outputs, camaraderie, knowing you were helping others, possibly saving lives or at least helping families who had lost loved ones by searching and new skills. If I could save just one life, I would be happy.

It was in 2010 that I did my swift water rescue training with them, literally training to pull people out of dangerous waters like man made weirs, rapids and various fast water hydrology features. The training had risks, it was dangerous and operating on weirs was full on, we had to do tethered swims into dangerous water only anchored by your colleague on dry land on the other end of the rope. It was a case of putting your life in someone else's hands if things went wrong. The personal floatation device (PFD) you were allocated had the ability through its harness, to operate a quick release mechanism.

In simple terms, on my PFD, if I got into trouble, I could choose to pull a chord on the front and float off in the torrent of white boiling water and swim into an Eddy (slower moving water) further downstream. It was pointless using your voice to call out on weirs, you would never be heard, it was, therefore, all down to hand signals which we practiced frequently mastering the language of key signs to prompt actions with colleagues. Getting it wrong could cost lives. We learnt how to span ropes across weirs to rescue bodies floating down stream, steering any body mass along the rope's diagonal axis, towards the bank and safety.

After I attained the International Rescue 3 qualification as a Swift Water Rescue Technician, those of us who were now qualified would go back to the same weir we had completed our training on, to practice, to keep our training current and be ready for that call to deploy and potentially save someone's life. In these training sessions, we would send a colleague over the weir all kitted up and then take turns swimming out on tethered lines to rescue them grabbing them by their PFD's shoulder straps and being hauled together, back to the riverbank by your teammates.

It was on one of these occasions I was the designated swimmer and was on standby to set about my rescue swim of the colleague (pseudo victim) being sent over the thunderous weir, tonnes of water cascading over the weir every second. I tapped the top of my head/safety helmet as a hand signal to the pseudo victim guy, about to wade into the calmer water above the weir, that all was ready and so did my colleague acting as my bank anchor who would also haul me in if I got into trouble.

I watched my colleague above the weir, start floating towards and down the weir and then descend the manmade slope of speeding water. I needed to time my swim perfectly in order to meet him in the middle of the river at exactly the same time. There is a lot to think about, the angle of your swim is key too as the force of water sends you at a down water trajectory, you also have to master your swim rate in order to reach him at the right moment in the furious water. I dived off the bank and started the swim, front crawl, a lot harder than being in a pool, I had a full dry suit on and a fully laden PFD with a cow-tail on the back attached to a float rope. The cow-tail was a stringy bungee rope attached by a carabiner to my PFD harness and the back of the quick release mechanism.

As I neared the supposed victim, he was waving his arms, to replicate drowning and fear, wildly above his head. As he came off the boil line and through the white mass of waves, something wasn't right, the rope attached to my cow-tail was pulling me down and I had trouble keeping my head above water, this wasn't normal, there is usually plenty of rope to give you flexibility and as the rope is light and designed to float it doesn't interfere with the rescue. My head was being pulled under and it was because of tension on the rope.

At this stage, your training kicks in and I aborted the rescue to concentrate on me, I was now the one in serious trouble and this wasn't a drill, it was very much suddenly for real. I instinctively pulled my quick release toggle on the front of my PFD. This part of the harness is essentially a belt around the

51

middle of the PFD that once you pull it, releases the whole belt and cow-tail and in effect the float rope attached to your bank team mate is left with just that part of your harness, the swimmer is then on their own to swim in the fast flowing water and to try and use knowledge of hydrology features to find a safe haven such as an eddy.

Shockingly, pulling my quick release toggle didn't work and whilst my belt had gone floppy and was no longer attached at the front of my PFD, it didn't release from my harness as intended. At the same time, my head was now completely submerged, I was not going to hold my breath much longer and needed a solution, time seemed to slow down. I was thinking clearly, running through remaining options, I knew I didn't have long. My teammate could have let go but in the mass of white water, he couldn't see the difficulty I was now in or hear me over the deafening noise. I am sure the dance of the flaming arseholes crossed my mind but this was not the time to compare crisis situations but at least my arse wasn't on fire.

I thought quickly, retracing in my mind what the cause might be. I concluded that when I dived in, the rope must have tangled around my ankle but things were becoming crucial, I was running out of air and desperately wanted to take a breath of oxygen. I had just this one hope before I became a real victim and that hope was to try and roll my body in the water, hopefully releasing the rope looped around my ankle but I didn't have time to roll both ways I had a choice…roll left or roll right.

I went with my gut instinct and rolled left, luckily, the right way but it had been a 50:50 decision. As soon as I completed the roll, I took in lungful's of air as I went over, the rope that had tethered me instantly floated away from my ankle, as did the whole of my quick release system, as I floated off downstream now gasping for air. It was with relief, after engaging my front crawl, that I saw the opportunity for safety and steered my weakened body into an eddy. Potentially a life or death decision but the right decision.

Again, I remembered a very wealthy client once telling me in my early days as a graduate, it is better to be able to make a decision, even if it is the wrong one than not at all.

As I stared back at Larry, oblivious to what his last few sentences had been, I now knew I needed to make a decision following the Dr Vegas medical regarding my symptoms as to whether to have a sigmoidoscopy investigation. Whilst this was totally different to the search and rescue incident, this could be an equally serious situation and required action. I promised Larry I would think about it.

I, however, continued to feel good, I continued playing veterans hockey and was going to the gym twice a week to get in shape. I continued a busy social life at work and at home and was loving life. There couldn't be much wrong with me, could there?

I reviewed the medical report from Dr Vegas which arrived from the medical provider, setting out in a summary section at the front of the report, my clean bill of health but suggesting I might want to look at the camera option sigmoidoscopy, to know exactly where the blood in my stools might have come from. I pondered this for a few minutes and instantly made a decision, I phoned the medical company and booked the first available appointment.

It then played on my mind, I still had occasional blood in my stool, a tiny bit of dull pain in my side and if I am honest, when the letter arrived from the hospital confirming my appointment for day surgery without an anaesthetic, highlighting their caveated set of risks, I started thinking about it more. According to the leaflet, one in 15,000 risk dying from a procedure without anaesthetic, sounded high to me.

Around this time, I had an away trip booked with some industry colleagues which involved each paying £100 and whoever wanted to go jumping on a train, bus or plane to an unknown destination. We would then all book into a hostel or hotel and then hit the bars. The trip in May 2016 was to Dublin and it was brilliantly organised and executed. We did the Jameson museum/factory getting well oiled on Jameson, ginger and lime. We then hired this road-going vehicle which has a driver, no engine but instead 16 peddle stations facing each other in pairs, to power it, in real terms that meant us.

It had a back seat for those not peddling and an air speaker which we could use to link in our phones to blast out some tunes. It was hard work, a heavy vehicle to propel around the centre of Dublin and it was a pub-crawl. So as we meandered around Dublin, with the exception of the driver, we gradually got more and more hammered. Down the middle of the vehicle was a walkway which we used as a dancing area. We were the centre of attention as members of the public and drivers looked on amused or dumb struck as we partied hard, letting our hair down. It was great, I loved it and it was what I needed to take my mind off things and the medical issues. I mentioned my pending investigative test to a few close friends on the trip but it was becoming less of a worry in my mind. I was having a ball and a positive time, I was 44 and far too young to be seriously ill, most of my friends agreed.

Chapter 10
Let's Get Serious, May 2016

The initial consultation with a bowel surgeon was at the hospital in Hereford in May, the word surgeon perhaps makes one more pessimistic than seeing a GP and the fact you are going to be in theatre on the day of attendance for the operation. The last time I had been to theatre was for my knee operation. The surgeon, Dr Amos, was, I estimated, about my age, olive skin, dark hair, knowledgeable and confident in his skill area. With a confident easiness, he took time to set out what type of things he would be looking for and then explained that the procedure was without an anaesthetic and that it may be a little uncomfortable at times.

My brain suddenly shouted out '…wait a minute…no anaesthetic!' Dr Amos outlined that I should only experience discomfort but no pain and that it was an easier procedure without anaesthetic but that there were risks with any surgery, for example of something going wrong and he set out these various risks too. The procedure was called a flexible sigmoidoscopy and I would be booked in for day surgery in July 2016. The conversation made me slightly worried, I thought, how big could this camera be and also perhaps, it wasn't too late for me to pull out.

I walked away with a leaflet which set out the risks described earlier, I skimmed through it, in short a 1 in 15,000 chance of death, a 1 in 1,000 chance of complications. Was I a man or mouse, I needed to just get through the process and out the other side and stop over analysing. Besides, I had a nice holiday in Northern Cyprus to look forward to in August, somewhere I had always wanted to go to and the procedure was set for July, so by August, I would, hopefully, have the all clear and could enjoy my holiday even more.

The next time I met Larry for a quick beer, I described the impending procedure, he was very interested and keen to learn about this metal snake that would be moving slowly up my back passage after lubrication. 'You lucky bastard', he kept saying, his eagerness to experience the same written all over his face, to Larry this was a sexual experience money couldn't buy easily.

The day of the operation came around soon enough, it would be performed by Dr Amos at the Herefordshire Private Hospital, and sure enough, I had been allocated my own en suite in the hospital ward. As instructed, I donned my dark blue and white checked patient gown and got to know the ward nurse looking after me, a petite woman who seemed to have her arms full, looking after numerous patients. The nurse explained she would reappear with a trainee (if I didn't mind the trainee assisting with the initial procedure?).

Mmmmm, what initial procedure? I pondered as the nurse continued to explain that the initial procedure was that they would need to give me an enema, to clear my bowels completely before surgery. I thought how embarrassing that might be, as possible scenarios of things going wrong in front of the trainee nurse flashed through my mind. It was a case of 'I am here now' and I didn't see that I had the option to say no, even if I did end up redecorating the room in front of an audience possibly wrecking a trainee nurse's medical career, scarring her for life.

Besides, people have to learn somewhere so why not on me, so I said, "Sure, why the hell not!" not really appreciating what was about to happen.

Shortly after my confirmation to be an exhibit, the female version of the Chuckle brothers walked in with what looked like a plastic bottle of wood glue, with a pointy nozzle on one end. I was asked to lie on my side and get my knees up towards my chin (I'd had heard that phrase before!). I pondered whether the Chuckle sisters knew Dr Gelardo and whether this was him getting me back for switching to a new medical provider all those years ago, or whether a few of the lads at work were getting me back. Perhaps, it was Digger finally seeking revenge for attempts on his life. As the more experienced of the Chuckle sisters inserted the nozzle and squeezed the contents up my back passage (a strange burning sensation, rippling around my colon), I spotted the trainee Chuckle sister looking on with gleeful appreciation. If I had thought about this beforehand, I could have got some tattoos done on each arse cheek saying 'Nurse training in progress'. Not the most enlightening experience for me, I can tell you, but after eight minutes, I didn't care, I was in and out of the en suite like the roadrunner, the irritant clearing my bowels as planned. Thankfully, the Chuckle sisters left me alone for that bit.

Eventually, two theatre nurses arrived to collect me, by which time I was on my bed ready to be wheeled into the operating room, emptied of matter and apologising profusely for any noxious gases that may still be permeating through the room from the en suite. These two were very nice ladies, kitted out in dark-blue theatre gowns, their face masks pulled down around their necks and seemed very professional unlike the Chuckle sisters, who had probably gone to compare notes on the cause and effect of shoving squeezy bottles up my arse.

There is a slight apprehension being wheeled towards an operating theatre, along corridors and then in a lift and eventually, into the operating room itself. Once there, I was interested in the setup of the room with its amazing air, spotlessly cleaned surfaces, I marvelled at seeing all those machines around me and people in masks but the team set me at ease and again, I was lying on my side with my knees up to my chin. I smirked again, the fact this could be the perfect wind up by my mates or even this surgeon perhaps knew Dr Gelardo, he was definitely getting his own back because I had swapped medical providers, I was sure of it. To my relief, the whole procedure was on a very large HD TV in front of me and the camera was more like a thin technical snake than your regular SLR, I was relieved but still not so sure I wanted it inside me. All that was missing was the popcorn, as I settled in for the ride and HD cinema experience.

All was going well as he lubed up his metal snake like tool and with a gentle reminder for me to stay relaxed, inserted the lengthy object and proceeded to take a tour of my colon and up towards my bowel. I thought of Larry being envious about this bit and managed a brief smile. All looked good on screen from my perspective and I was just thinking I am surely wasting their time, when I noticed him hovering over something on the screen then zooming in.

I knew it in the moment, as the focus on the TV screen sharpened and he zoomed in, but it was when he suddenly said, "It is a really good job you are having this procedure today," that

57

even the nurses started looking towards the image. On screen was what looked like the Malvern Hills with some signs of blood around the base. Whatever it was, I knew it wasn't right and putting two and two together, I assumed it was probably where the blood was potentially coming from.

"I need to take some immediate biopsies," was his next response, "you will feel some tugging but it shouldn't be painful as the nerve endings are different internally." The surgeon took two samples from the Malvern Hills, the position seemed halfway along my colon and then checked as far as my bowel for anything else but there wasn't anything more to see. Dr Amos was right, I didn't feel too much pain with the biopsies but it was very uncomfortable when he pushed on as far as he could to go looking towards the bowel. I was having to breathe through the uncomfortableness, this was a new sensation for me and then he extracted his camera and it was over.

On getting back to my room, I was promptly given my pre-ordered lunch and was already dressed and ready to leave shortly after downing the food. After all, I had had no anaesthetic, I felt good and full of energy. It was then the main Chuckle sister who reappeared and shut the door behind her. *Hello*, I thought, *she wants me to do a questionnaire on how good her trick with the glue bottle was or wants to tell me how pretty my bottom is privately*. I was just considering telling her I would give her five out of ten for surprise and six out of ten for effort for the glue bottle trick, when she said the surgeon wanted to see me and my wife both at the same time, perhaps when my wife was picking me up later in the day. I explained that as my wife, Claudia, didn't finish work until 5 p.m., I could actually get home quicker with my dad at, say, 2 p.m.

"No," she said firmly, "Dr Amos wants to see you and your wife, 5 p.m. is fine." I saw a seriousness and a large degree of sincerity in her eyes as she spoke, before she turned and left me alone in the room.

I was really annoyed, I felt great and now I would have to wait until 5 p.m. It felt like it had been an eternity when Claudia eventually arrived. I had watched numerous daytime soaps and quiz shows and then bang on 5 p.m., the surgeon, Dr Amos, came in and asked us both to sit down. I thought he looked more serious than any of the times I had seen him before and his first sentence certainly didn't disappoint.

"Following your procedure this morning, I think this is a very serious diagnosis, clearly, we need to wait for the results of the biopsy but you will need a CT scan right away."

I countered with various questions such as, "Could it be a haemorrhoid, pile or just a lump or is it cancer, is it treatable?" The medical profession are well trained in their responses to patients, in his opinion, we needed to wait for the results but in his professional view, all things considered, it looked very serious and yes, this could be cancer.

We agreed to meet again once the results were known, he then said, "You may want to stay in the room for a while."

I knew where he was going with this comment, he expected me to be emotional and maybe want time to have quiet moment having received hard news.

"We are fine, let's go," I said with positivity and a quick adaption to the news I had just received. Nobody had told me I was dying albeit I accepted there was clearly something wrong but I was a survivor and the positive attitude kicked in from that moment. I was also keen to get the results, this may not be as bad as it seemed was the thought I clinged onto, surely, the scan would prove everyone wrong. I felt largely good, I was a fit hockey player, running regularly albeit on receiving such news your mind does start to suggest that pain I had been experiencing in that region of the body, might be linked to this all along and not as a result of being struck by the hockey ball which had hurtled into me at high speed.

Initially, I told very few people around me, my parents and close pals only, they were all concerned but appreciated it was very early days and may not be bad news until I had the results.

The next step was the CT scan, which was, again, at the Herefordshire Private Hospital, but in the back of a large lorry parked at the back of the hospital. The lorry apparently tours different hospitals nationwide, so ends up in a different location from day to day and it is a bit like entering a spaceship. The hardest part with a scan where they need to light up your abdomen, pelvis and thorax with contrast dye, is that they need to get dye into your blood stream quickly as you go through the scanner. The only way they can administer the dye in quick time is via a very large needle inserted into a vein on your arm.

The male nurse was friendly enough and had me lie on the bed adjacent to the scanner, while he cleaned the inside of my arm and said, "Sharp scratch," (which for me on this occasion felt like a knife had been inserted into my arm).

Christ, I thought, *how uncomfortable,* as the needle linked to the various tubes pierced my skin and was positioned into the vein, I was then told to place my hands above my head which was even more uncomfortable. This was all new and I had bent my arm slightly when the needle was inserted, more painful as a result in my view, today I would hardly notice an injection and had learnt to keep my vein as straight as possible. Just before the third trip through the scanning hoop (which looks like some alien experiment contraption), the dye goes into your blood stream making you feel like you pissed yourself, put it this way, I had to pause and think whether I had flooded the scanner.

Overall, it was a relatively quick process and largely without pain. As I walked out of the scanner room, I caught a glimpse of two other nurses/medical staff sat in front of screens looking at the 3D images of my body. I would have liked to have known what was in front of them but I didn't ask and they didn't exchange any glances my way either, they were giving nothing away.

I didn't have to wait too long for the results, the surgeon wanted to bring the appointment forward a few days which was a bit surprising and again, I found myself back in the hospital, accompanied by my wife to get a debrief on the biopsies and scans from Dr Amos. After a short wait of form filling and magazine flicking in the waiting room, we were ushered into see Dr Amos in a small consultation room. I didn't know what to expect, facts are facts and I just hoped it was a polyp or some lost precious ring I might have swallowed from my childhood that simply needed removing. Briefly looking down at his notes, Dr Amos then looked up and at me, staring sternly straight into my eyes and said with a low matter of fact tone, "The bowel biopsies have come back suspicious of cancer but are not conclusive, but in my view this looks to be a cancer, upper rectal or recto-sigmoid cancer."

I remained silent for a moment, trying to detect any empathy in his voice, and then politely responded in as calm a voice I could muster, "How aggressive, on a scale of 1–3?"

He paused, looked right into my eyes for a second time still with a serious expression and said, "A STAGE 4." I thought for a second or two, gradually processing this news and its impact on my day, but all I could think of was the fact I hadn't given him 1–4 options, only options 1–3. Before I could think any further with my train of thought, he continued, "The scan also showed some black spots on either side of your liver, which would indicate that if it is indeed an aggressive cancer, it has unfortunately had time to spread, the bowel and liver are closely linked, and the liver is one of the major organs bowel cancer can spread to. I would recommend you see an oncologist right away." I was just sat there listening and processing, absorbing but strategizing in my mind at the same time…

…one of the things I thought was, 'What the fuck is an oncologist?'

Somewhere in my brain, a voice was saying, this is different, you do risk, like challenge, we will attack it…but this is as big as they come. This was an even more serious conversation than the last meeting with this guy, I felt well so it is very difficult to be told you are actually very sick and then very frustrating not to be able to solve the issue there and then. All I could do was take his advice, listen and stay positive. I was keen to get a further view and asked to see the oncologist as soon as possible and I meant right away, I didn't want to wait. Claudia and I drove home and en route discussed the experience deciding we would both remain firmly positive for the sake of people around us especially my boys, Flynn and Josh, after all nothing was yet conclusive.

It would have been easy to take the last few days as negative knocks, serious episodes of life, a heavy issue that brings you down but I don't think like that, you have to make the best of a situation. I would not shirk my responsibility here.

I was lucky and got an appointment in Cheltenham to meet a Dr Jackson who had been sent my results and the appointment was scheduled for the next day. It made me think would an NHS patient have got an appointment that quickly, I felt I was fortunate. Dr Jackson was in his mid-50s by my estimation and a gentle, kindly spoken man, very considered in what he said, an intellectual type, conveying a well-experienced aura. I noticed immediately the focus had shifted from my bowel more to my liver.

After some pleasantries and being ushered to seats in his office, he began, "These are not so much spots but look to be tumours, bilobar liver metastases affecting both sides of your liver the largest being 5cm across, I am recommending we start you on chemotherapy immediately."

Chemotherapy, I thought, *Christ, I have heard of that, it's for people with serious cancer, I know people who have had chemotherapy and have died! It makes your hair fall out too.* It was dawning on me more and more, I was ill and even if I didn't feel ill, things like chemotherapy I expected would be no walk in the park. Dr Jackson went on to explain that liver metastases are cancerous tumours that have spread to the liver from a cancer that started in another place in the body.

This was yet another step up in the seriosity stakes, again I needed to adapt and search for the positives, which were becoming less and less evident. The only positive I could see was there must be a chance, no matter how remote, the fact they were putting me on chemo was a plus point. One of my first questions was, "Is this treatable, is there a positive prognosis?"

Clearly, this guy couldn't give a response with a definitive hopeful outcome. "Stanley," Dr Jackson started softly, "you need to know that this does look like a serious cancer which has had time to spread to your liver and both sides of your liver too and that whilst we will start targeting it with the chemotherapy, it may be inoperable. Given the positions of these tumours, you need to be realistic, this may not be a positive outcome for you," he winced his face as he spoke, his cheeks expressing some form of facial sympathy. "We will need to get you in for a liver biopsy right away."

I remember sitting there, Claudia wiping away a small tear trickling down her cheek and me challenging the emotion rising up within, I felt that internal heat you get with a pressure moment or when you have done something very bad perhaps, such as you have just opened the mail to find a speeding notice but 100 mph in a 30! My mind was racing to adapt, I needed to be in control, I needed to take a path to beat this but as I stared back at Dr

Jackson, scanning his face trying to work out what I was feeling the primary thought was, where were the positives here…

The positives I quickly concluded were this: 1) no one has told me I am dying yet albeit this was pretty close 2) it could be worse and have spread to more organs 3) why put me on chemo unless there was a chance 4) I was a fighter, new challenge and new battle, game on, I needed a new focus anyway, life was challengeless currently.

You walk away from a meeting like that feeling bruised somewhere deep inside, the confusing thing for me was I felt pretty much fine, although your mind starts to say, 'See, I told you that pain above your hip was something serious…' but you have to be very focused and just don't listen to the negatives from your mind!

I was in a separate car to Claudia driving back from Cheltenham to Hereford, I needed to discuss this and with the hands-free telephone cutting out the stereo, turned to those close friends around me in a series of phone calls as I drove. I was starting to draw down positivity from those I knew would provide it, although it was interesting how I noticed the reactions of those around me to the news, this sequence of events was a shock for them also.

Chapter 11
Attempt Two and Three

I love my mates, I love people and colourful characters which all of my friends are and some of the times we had have been memorable, sometimes for the wrong reasons.

In about 2005, I jointly invested in a speedboat with Fred, a long-term mate who worked for the fire brigade, Fred was always the peak of fitness with Jason Statham looks. She wasn't the biggest boat or completely sea worthy but she promised to give us a thrill, having a powerful Evanrude engine on her stern. There were no speed or engine dials with the boat, just a veneer or fake wooden dashboard, a steering wheel and her power was engaged with a lever on the right-hand side of the driver's seat. We named the boat Lady Penelope, something about her reminded me of the Thunderbirds series and I got a pal in a signage business to run and then print some name designs for the boat along with a James Bond type female silhouette, he came up with the outline of a sexy female in stilettos holding a gun. In addition, we had the boat's number S86 in a 'Herby goes bananas' style transfer positioned on the bow, ahead of the wind shield. In her original metallic brown above waterline, cream lower half and with her fake leather seats and now cream transfers she looked the typical 40 something midlife crisis toy and…she probably was!

The first few launches didn't go well, the fuel line had perished and on turning the engine a few times, it ruptured and sprayed Fred with the fine mix of unleaded petrol mixed with marine oil, she was literally going nowhere until we replaced the fuel line.

The problems didn't stop there. On another occasion, we adjusted the steel wires that ran over four pulleys located at each corner of the boat's inside, these are used to connect to the steering and then connect also with the outboard engine which essentially is the means of steering the boat. Fred, as the more practical amongst us, did most of the work, we took it in turns to crawl into the dark corners of the boat resetting the steel wires and set out to tighten the steering by pulling the wires taut and rewrapping the wires around the steering column.

Once we had completed the maintenance, I was hoping to have first go in Lady Penelope that day, we had brought our families down to the beach all of us camping on the Gower for a few days with the kids eager to get out in Lady Penelope. During the stay, each morning, I would drive my 4x4 Nissan down the sand to the sea's edge and Fred and I would take the trailer off the vehicle and manually run the trailer with Lady P on it into the sea until she floated free from the trailer. We would reconnect the trailer to the 4x4 and I would drive back up the beach and leave both the Nissan X-Trail and trailer in the parking area some 300 meters away and run on foot back to the sea and where Fred, up to his waist in water, was holding the boat, just off shore.

On this occasion, the works we had done to the steering had been at the campsite and so having dropped the boat into the calm waters of Oxwich Bay, it really was our first opportunity to test her improved steering.

To my disappointment, after the effort of assisting with the repair, hauling Lady P into the water and then parking the 4x4 and trailer and running half way down the beach, Fred, to my amazement, had taken the opportunity to put his wife and kids in the boat and set off out into the bay.

'How nice, no communication and now off they go, I'll just stay on the beach then!' I was thinking, swearing under my breath. A split second later, I was literally thinking I am so glad that wasn't me in the boat, and I couldn't stop laughing.

To Fred's utter dismay, when he turned left to head out into the bay, the boat turned in totally the opposite direction towards the cliffs and he was struggling to correct it with limited manoeuvring space between the boat's position and the rocky cliffs and hidden underbelly of rock formations just below the sea.

Whilst it is dangerous not to be in control of a boat, Fred was a capable guy, a fireman and trained helmsman in search and rescue. Relatively quickly, as he tempered his speed to the dawning situation, he realised his error after numerous attempts trying to correct the opposite effect the steering column was having to his every move. Unbeknown to Fred, at the time, he had wound the steel wires the wrong way around the steering column, meaning a turn to port was now a turn to starboard and so on. All in all, as I stood there in creases of laughter, it was very funny and I was glad it wasn't me having to cope with that, with a hangover too, I am not sure I would have worked it out but these things are sent to try us, we find ourselves in situations suddenly and it is about adaption. It was an important lesson.

On another outing with Lady P, we were again camping on the Gower and Lady Penelope was not running at all smoothly and after the usual tinkering, the engine didn't work. Fred and I began arguing fiercely mainly on two points 1) of my lack of input into the maintenance and 2) from my perspective, that we should just pay a proper maintenance bloke to repair her as whatever was wrong was beyond Fred's usually tip-top solutions.

Between arguments, we got the engine going on the campsite and decided to launch her once more off the beach. This time, Fred patiently waited for me to return from parking the vehicle and trailer and we set off out to sea but unfortunately, at a quarter of the normal speed (the most Penelope could muster), as much as we tried to bring the revs up, Lady Penelope resisted, offering momentary glimpses of her potential and then dying again. It was a mile off shore that Lady P stopped completely and fell completely silent. It is very easy if you are not trained to panic especially with a wind blowing you further out to sea. People can get into serious trouble at sea if you don't know what you are doing and people break down in boats frequently with dire consequences not knowing how to react. Once out of sight, in a small craft at sea, you are difficult to locate by rescuers without a radar beacon/signal. A boat as light as Lady P would soon be drifting into the Atlantic and be difficult to spot from a helicopter in the vast expanse of ocean.

Fred and I were both boat-trained rescuers and weren't worried, we simply carried on arguing like brothers about whose fault this actually was. I dropped anchor to fix our position to prevent the boat drifting and it was a case of engine cover off and let's try and do a Fred special and fix the boat. We both opened a can of Fosters to calm ourselves down. Initial attempts to fix the problem did not work but Fred had a hunch as to the problem and with it being a calm sea, he decided what we needed was a good old-fashioned spanner, opting to swim back to shore while I manned the boat.

I watched Fred for ages gradually becoming a faint dot as he swam against the wind as I sat drinking my beer on the side of the boat as it swayed gently against the anchor chain. It must have taken him 30 minutes to swim back to shore then run up the beach to retrieve a spanner. It was another 30-minute swim back to the boat! I admired the perseverance, the confidence Fred had, I had those qualities but Fred had bags of both and it reminded me I should engage both more often.

During the long period Fred was gone, I befriended a very welsh jet skier.

"All right, Butt? Need a tow?" were his first words as he throttled down the jet ski and fell off into the water beside it, still gripping the handles of the jet ski.

I said, "We are having a few engine dramas, mate, just keep an eye on us, buddy, if we are still here in an hour, we may well need a tow!"

"Right you are, Butt, I'll be skimming the bay," and with that, he throttled the engine with high revs and the jet ski dragged him off with half his arse cheeks hanging out of his shorts. I was in stitches watching him trying to re-position himself on the jet ski and address his malfunctioning wardrobe issues.

Fred seemed a bit knackered as I hauled his muscular frame back into the boat. He'd swam best part of 2 miles without a life jacket and as I resumed to my trusted can of Fosters, he produced from his wet suit a very large monkey wrench. Unfortunately, this didn't work and we were both getting annoyed with the time we were wasting and when, in life, a strategy needs to be implemented or doesn't work, you adjust it or maximise your alternative options. So, with that, I waved at Butt Cheeks as he shot past on his jet ski. Sure enough, he obliged by coming over and unintentionally toppling off his jet ski, treading water alongside our boat.

"Right boys," he said in a Swansea accent as he tried not to swallow sea water, "you throw me a rope, I'll tow you back in." It is worth pointing out at this stage that you always throw the rescuer the rope in a situation like this, don't accept his rope or he can claim part of the value of your vessel as salvage. In Lady Penelope's case, that would not be a vast sum of money and the rope might have been worth more but it's more the principle. That said in an emergency at sea, I don't think you would be that bothered who gave who a rope or how much it cost.

Butt Cheeks from Swansea, revved his engine several times, the rope went taut and slowly, we started to move. (Don't worry...I had pulled the anchor). The problem was with the full weight of the boat, two of us supping our cans of Fosters and the sheer weight of hauling Butt Cheeks out of the water, the jet ski was struggling, its engine squealing with the strain. Butt Cheeks was not getting out of the water but was being dragged at an awkward angle alongside his jet ski. His shorts gradually slipped all the way down his arse and ended up just above his knees. I don't think he noticed, he was too busy trying to keep his mouth above the waterline.

It was embarrassing being rescued back to shore by a jet-ski in front of all the holiday makers and our families but I was relieved to be heading back to shore, we had adjusted our strategy avoided a catastrophe at sea. Manning a broken vessel a mile out to sea isn't too much fun, however watching Butt Cheeks try and get to a standing position on his jet ski was priceless. Sadly, a few hours later, while we recovered Penelope to our trailer, Butt Cheeks was still trying to get his jet ski going again, it had seemingly blown its engine following the strain of the rescue. I waved, he didn't wave back.

So against a background of regular maintenance issues with Lady Penelope, we soldiered on trying to enjoy her, usually over summer months, when she was going well, she went very well and she looked the part. A real 80s boat which would look out of place as a tender in some posh, large yacht marina or rocking up to a yupee pub via a pier.

An invite came from Digger to have a boating lads' weekend at his relatively new holiday home. Digger was doing very well with his businesses, expanding, buying new companies and doubling profits overnight. The house was a beauty, probably one of the nicest in Pembrokeshire, a large sprawling property nestled into the hillside overlooking the Haven Estuary, set in 8 acres of Rhododendrons, with sweeping pathways down to its own pier, boathouse and crane for lowering tenders into the water. Without hesitation, Fred and I accepted the invitation and gave Lady Penelope a thorough going over, packed the water skis and crates of beer and headed off. Due to Fred's work commitments, we were a day behind the others and on arrival, we were greeted by a very hungover Digger complaining about a forfeit challenge he had lost the night before. The forfeit being he now had the unfortunate humiliation to be towed naked around the bay behind his brother.

Anchored on a mooring buoy, just off the pier was Digger's 8m RIB with a powerful Evanrude 200hp. Not many people were allowed to helm her but I was one of the privileged few along with Brad, Digger's brother. It was a very funny sight seeing a naked knee boarder being towed a lot faster than he wanted for a lot longer than he would prefer past families on the stoney shoreline, the kids waving initially then clearly saying to their parents, "Daddy, that man is naked!" When Brad brought the RIB to a standstill, he received a proper bollocking from Digger.

That evening, Digger bailed to bed at some ridiculously early hour, much to Fred and my displeasure, it was our first night to let our hair down with the group, get to know them. Surely this was the height of rudeness, Digger was the host after all. We did, however, drink plenty with the guys in his absence and the collective consensus was that Digger had bailed too early and a further forfeit was in order.

Digger had kindly given up the master bedroom en suite for Fred and I to sleep in and he himself, being the selfless kind fellow he is, had taken to a camp bed in the dressing room just off the en suite. It was there he was out for the count snoring for England, probably dreaming about his naked water skiing and hoping he didn't meet any of the families he had seen that day as he flew past naked yelling, "Stop, you bastards!"

My plan was simple, his forfeit would be a daring mission to collectively carry his camp bed while he slept in the peaceful haven of his sleeping bag to an ice cold bath and tip him in. Like a well-drilled commando raid on an dangerous x-ray combatant at night, we all tip-toed up the stairs along the landing, putting in the odd forward roll for comedy effect and diving forward doorway to doorway. I was the raid leader and we had rehearsed our roles. After filling the bath positioned on its own in the middle of the expansive en suite, we gathered on either side of the camp bed and the snoring Digger (his water ski dreams were about to get a lot wetter). With him still snoring, we carried Digger on his camp bed to the en suite, he was still sleeping and snoring like a baby. I think there must be a wake up reflex in humans just past a 45-degree angle as he woke fractionally before he hit the icy depths of the bathtub.

"Ah, ah, fuck, fuck, you cunts, ah, ah, that's cold, you bastards, ah, ah, my chest…oh, oh, oh, that's cold…!" I don't think I have seen someone try and get to their feet so quickly after waking up. By the time he did, we had fled the scene.

It was only then that I really thought about the shock issue, the resting body at a low calm heart rate suddenly being thrust into a potentially hypothermic state of high heart rate and immediate shock. Digger might be having a heart attack here his heart rate having gone from 65 beats per minute to 200! This was another irresponsible subconscious attempt on his life and he wasn't happy. How had I nearly killed him twice, little did I know, the worse was to come the next day.

Digger wasn't talking to me for most of the morning, Fred and I were in Lady Penelope drinking and smoking rollies (away from the fuel but still reckless given Lady P's lack of health and safety), Digger and the other guys in the RIB doing water sports, mainly knee boarding. We had all then decamped to a pub for lunch, having sampled the local seafood cuisine and a few beers. The race back to the ski area in front of the house from the pub mooring was epic, a couple of miles of flat water the 200hp up against good fun Lady Penelope, so light in comparison with a smaller 60hp Evanrude (probably the largest engine she would take without flipping over and killing us at full tilt). The RIB was considerably more the heavy hulk, so needed its massive power unit to give it speed, it felt a close race but the RIB just beat us back albeit I was sure the ride in Lady P was more fun, living on the edge of sensibility. For the remainder of the afternoon, we continued to do water sports, Fred and I, happy in Lady Penelope, rejoicing in the fact she had not yet succumbed to a maintenance issue.

Later that afternoon, a deep mist descended over the water ski area and it was difficult to see the RIB some 200 metres away but we could hear her growling, accelerating, powering down, such a beautiful sound of a well-tuned deep sounding engine. We ventured in their direction and as they were in neutral, we pulled alongside. Digger seemed more ready to forgive me for the near heart attack the previous night and plus, his lips were no longer blue, so he suggested he might try water skiing off the back of Lady Penelope as her wake was less prolific, it should be easier than skiing behind the RIB. Fred would hop into the RIB for half an hour for some knee boarding and we all agreed we would keep a fair way apart to avoid the issues with the reducing visibility and the mist.

All was well for a while, Digger had a blast driving Lady P and we had a good chat about the heart attack incident, I promised I would never try to unintentionally or intentionally kill him again but we were mates living on the edge of risk constantly but loving life, we both agreed I would make more effort.

It was time for Digger to water ski, so I hauled out Penelope's bright yellow skis. I felt honoured to show someone Lady Penelope was as good as any other boat, could behave and give some serious pleasure to a genuine water sports enthusiast. Digger dropped over the side using a few front crawl strokes to get to the handle of the towrope. Unlike more modern boats, Lady P had two anchor points either side of the outboard engine, connected to this was a rigid frame/rope which floated, this was then connected by a carabena to a towrope which also floated. I would guess, at-full stretch, the rope was 15–20 metres from the boat. I gently came out of neutral and nudged Lady P forward towards the clear water ahead, the towrope gathering up slack.

At this point, you should have a spotter on board to always keep eyes on the water skier. We were breaking the rules, still I had my kill chord connected to my wrist from the ignition unit, which, in the event I lost control or got thrown overboard, the engine would cut immediately. There had been a horrendous and very sad incident on the south coast reported in the media of a family on a similar RIB to Digger's being thrown overboard as it suddenly hit full speed in a turn. The boat then continued to plough into the family in ever-tighter circles as they waved helplessly in the water, the engine still powering hard with no one at the helm. People lost their lives, a propeller is a hugely dangerous part of the boat below water, never seen but spinning at an incredible speed. Accidents around water often happen quickly.

Digger was, himself, getting ready for his run, his knees to his chest the two water skis in between his legs, the ideal scenario is for the skier to get the ski tips vertical between his knees, at which point he would say, "Gun it," and I would then go full throttle, in a straight line. On feeling the force of the boat through his arms, Digger would almost do a forward roll pushing down on his skis, to a stand up position at which point I would throttle back to 12–15 knots and maintain this speed, Digger then standing up right carving behind the boat.

"Gun it," I heard from behind me loud and clear, and I hit the throttle lever forward as far as it would go. Everything was going well for a second or two, Digger was emerging from the water, when at full speed, the steering suddenly spun, sending Lady Penelope into a dangerously sharp turn at a very high speed, I wasn't myself in danger of being thrown overboard, as Lady P's seats were like low Recarro seats, quite fitted and on the floor with my legs flat on the boat floor in front of me but I suddenly had absolutely no control of the steering, something had massively failed.

The boat was now coming straight again of its own accord and heading full force towards Digger, head on, it would cover the ground in no time. In a split second decision, I pulled the kill chord and the boat speed died immediately, decelerating very quickly and eventually, gliding the few remaining yards to a shocked Digger in silence. I anchored and tried to piece what had occurred together and explain the events to Digger.

In an eerily echoing way, the events on the Gower with the steering going wrong, were repeating themselves, again, the steel wire that loops around the steering column and four pulleys in each corner, had somehow sheared off its mounting completely, resulting in a destabilisation of the tension on the steel wire required to handle the boat. Any movements I made on the steering wheel would have no effect. I knew this could have been very serious, my training had kicked in just in time.

On realising another attempt had been made on his life, albeit unintentionally, Digger didn't seem too happy again. I could see why and sympathised.

I pondered, *I am immune to these dangers now, I am invincible!*

How wrong could I be.

Chapter 12
Wearing My Heart on My Sleeve

The liver biopsy procedure, from what I read from the leaflet that arrived with my appointment confirmation, was another day procedure and I had been booked in for a Tuesday in July at Hereford County Hospital, department of Gastroenterology. A Dr Allen would be performing the biopsy, a procedure which was relatively new to Hereford Hospital. The thought of someone taking part of your liver away did play on my mind, I tried to imagine what sensations I would experience. Another leaflet I read went into more detail about the fact that there was less percentage probability of an operation being offered on a secondary cancer which had spread to the liver. Once I got the gist of the paragraph, I ignored it. It was a negative.

When the day arrived, I got to the hospital ward, literally as the doors opened and the ward staff were arriving for work, I was just so eager to get this done and crossed off the list. After more form filling of key personal details, allergies and medical history, I got allocated a gown and bed on the ward. This was a narrow ward and largely empty apart from me and an elderly gentleman in for what I presumed was a lung biopsy. I felt a bit sorry for him as he was on his own, and I pondered how that must feel to have no one there with you.

As usual, Claudia was by my side, making positive conversation between interludes on her iPad. I wouldn't have been able to read a book or iPad, my mind was too focused on being ready for the procedure. Thankfully, it wasn't long before I got wheeled into another theatre room, again I found myself nervously surveying the room and the bits of medical kit within it, these rooms were like something from the next century to me, so high-tech and with beautifully clear air, there was just the one surgeon this time and one theatre nurse. Dr Allen explained he would first anaesthetise the area below my ribs after he had marked it out and some of this anaesthetic would then drip onto the liver and then they would go for the biopsies with a large needle like device with pinchers. There was a demonstration of the sound I would hear of the implement taking the biopsy, to me it sounded pretty much the same as a pair of garden secateurs, snipping away at out of control garden stems.

According to Dr Allen, apparently the pain sensation I would experience would be different to, say, cutting sensations on your skin, sensations internally were not the same, the nerve endings are completely different but it would feel uncomfortable. How do you mentally prepare for an unknown, new, very strange experience, expected to be slightly unpleasant but overall a manageable experience? I just hit it head on, confronted it. Dr Allen, sure enough, spent a few minutes drawing pictures on my side with a marker pen and putting a big surgical pad on my side. Then, while I looked the other way, what I can only imagine was his one very large needle, bore all the way through my side anesthetising the area as it went. I could feel a combination of a burning sensation, stinging and then cold dribbling feeling which I assumed must be the liquid dripping onto my liver. I was then told to hold my breath while I felt this instrument pushing hard on my liver and then as I held my breath, an unusual and uncomfortable tugging sensation and a loud 'snip', the first biopsy was taken.

I didn't feel great, it was a bit like someone pressing on a bruise and tugging a section of it away but somewhere deep inside my body. He was scheduled to take two biopsies but after I had endured the second pressurising snipping procedure, he asked if he minded if he took three samples. I didn't really want to repeat this process but reluctantly, agreed. Before I knew it, I was back on the ward, being closely monitored for changes. The liver is the biggest vascular organ in the body and bleeding can start quite easily from the wound. I was told to remain as still as possible for most of the remainder of the day, which, for me, was hard to do, just lying there, starring at ceiling tiles, making idle chat. Thankfully, apart from a few low blood pressure readings, I was fine and much later that day, I left the hospital feeling a bit bruised.

The drive home was fine until we hit the farm track leading to the house. Every time the car hit a pothole, I would feel pain and I wished I had gotten the track fixed earlier in the year. I told Claudia to stop the car after the first few bounces and I got out and walked the remaining distance to the house.

It is slightly surreal when you have just had day surgery to then pop over to some friends for a catch up but that is exactly what we did, popping into to see great neighbours, Liam and Nina. Nina had suffered from serious illness in the past and was a strong believer in nutrition, it having been the helping hand in her recovery, massively tackling issues in a positive way and was keen to recommend to me her nutritionist, who incidentally specialised in cancer care. The nutritionist had a fellowship in cancer care, having worked with oncologists in America, where nutrition and medical science are more closely linked. I made some notes and wondered whether nutrition could make a difference for me? Liam is a great guy and on hearing my experience with the farm track having to walk because I could feel my bruised liver with every pothole, two days later, he sent his workman to fill the potholes, a lovely gesture.

The next day, I emailed the nutritionist Nina had recommended, I figured it could do no harm despite some reservations. I knew friends who were nutritionists and didn't see this recommendation as unique at the time but with my positive hat on, I engaged the contact. I am so glad I listened to Nina.

It was also time for my first visit from the health care at home team, in essence, the nurses who would be administering the chemo drugs to me. This was all completely new and I guess, overall, a bit daunting. You have to go on the attack though, not with the nurses but from the perspective of confronting new experiences. You have to take the attitude, OK, this is new but really how hard can it be, see it as an exciting challenge, you challenge yourself to deal with the task easily and move on.

The nurse was called Karen, a very friendly type who had been doing this type of nursing for 14 years or more and with military nursing experience overseas, we got on immediately. Karen explained that the start of a cycle of chemo started with my bloods being tested on the Tuesday at home, they would then be couriered to the hospital immediately from my driveway for testing, the quicker they arrived in a good state, the more accurate the results.

I struggled to appreciate the seriousness, while one nurse took my bloods a vehicle courier would be sat on my drive ready to whisk away the samples for testing. Provided all was well with the results, the following Thursday, I would be wired up to a drip via a cannula and given a proportion of the chemo drugs intravenously over the course of six hours. Why six hours? It is one nurse with no back up, if things go wrong by trying to force drugs in too quickly, it may not end well.

Initially, your mind thinks, "What the fuck…a needle taking blood on Tuesday and then two days later, a needle stuck in my arm for six hours?" You have to look for the positives and you really have to accept you are in a process which is for your benefit to try and make you well again, whether or not it succeeds is beside the point. You must hand your body over to medical science and let the experts get on with their jobs and do everything in your power to maximise your ability to assist them in every way to fully benefit from the medicine.

Karen took all my key readings, blood pressure, weight, temperature and then showed me how simple the taking of blood was. I had had bloods taken before; at the various consultations, the recently endured scope and biopsy operations but this was now going to be every two weeks, at home and for something that I had heard bad things about…chemotherapy. I think it kind of felt more of an elevated issue in my head. It wasn't and I needed not to be worried. Every blood test usually starts with the nurse saying, 'sharp scratch coming up' and there is, or is there? If there is, it is a minor prick of pain in the scheme of things.

After that initial scratch, if there is one, the pain is gone in a millisecond, the needle is horizontally sliding into your venous vein and you don't feel it. You are aware of the nurse maybe fiddling with the cannula to start filling vials with your blood but it is a painless process when you think about it. Before you know it, the needle is out and you are pressing down on a piece of gauze to stem any bleeding and then a small plaster goes on. I was told as a patient I would get to know my bloods really well and in detail. I learnt from Karen I would be given a treatment book which listed all the elements of my blood including things like a CEA (Carcinoembryonic antigen) score which shows the level of proteins being released from the cancer tumours into the bloodstream, spreading around my body.

Quite quickly, possibly the same day, Karen texted me to say, the bloods were in order for chemotherapy treatment. Karen would be wiring me up for the first time to give me chemo on Thursday. I had a look at the various blood headings and didn't understand any of the abbreviated names but I saw that my CEA (cancer tumour marker) score was 416. I asked Karen if this was exceptionally high and she confirmed it was. A normal healthy adult score is 3–4.

"What…three or four, mine is 416!" I was quite shocked. This was considerably more than the norm so it made me a bit down but the fight has to start somewhere and this was a challenge in my mind to now bring my CEA score down through my strategy.

I was more nervous perhaps because of the unknown but my attitude was resolutely to confront it, especially any hesitancy or fear in your mind and overcome those thoughts. Focus on something to look forward to beyond the treatment even if it is just something to eat or just relax and make sure you are comfortable.

I opted for an armchair in the lounge, after all, I could work on the laptop from there and watch TV over lunch breaks. As Karen set up the drip stand and opened her builders tool box of multitudes of medical items, she wanted me to soak my forearms in warm water in the sink. Karen explained it helps get the juicy veins up. It felt weird standing at the sink unit, staring out of the kitchen window with my arms submerged up to the elbow in warm water, I, however, made myself enjoy it, as I watched a greater spotted woodpecker dart between cider apple trees in the orchard beyond the window. When I was called back to the cooler air of the lounge, with its thick 18th century walls, I made myself comfortable and noticed the needle was a bigger one compared to say a blood needle for a blood test.

Karen explained, "It needs to sit in a vein for a long time allowing literally litres of chemicals to filter into your blood stream."

Karen was so gentle with the needle (a true pro) and once it was strapped down with tape where it pierced the skin and ran along the vein, I didn't notice any pain or any of the various drips going in. I just got on with life, work and being myself. I knew it was important never to lose sight of that. If you need the loo, you have to stand up and walk with the drip stand which is on wheels with the cannula and drugs all still attached. It is awkward at first but it is literally all fine, just a new process to get used to. Think of it as learning something new, a new thing you know how to do, there is a positive in everything. I remember that first time banging the drip stand into doors and skirting boards on the long walk to the downstairs loo, tangling myself up with the electrical and drip wires coming from the drip stand. I told myself I will become good at this and in no time at all, I truly was an expert at it. No matter how small a challenge, my viewpoint was to master it.

Perhaps the biggest surprise was when Karen announced that she needed to give me a certain injection for anti-sickness and offered to give me it through my stomach wall. As much as I have a positive outlook and had confronted injections and slotted it into a positive shelf in my mind, I didn't relish the thought of an injection in my stomach. Especially after having the liver biopsy two days before, I was at the point of too much to deal with in one day. If you don't ask you don't get, so I asked if there was another part of the body it could be injected into. We agreed the back of the arm and whilst it was a long injection needle and stung a lot, it was completely manageable. I know now what I didn't know then, that after experiencing several of these stinging injections, you need to remain very relaxed not tense and concentrate on calm breathing to limit the pain. It does work to channel that way of thinking when you are having it administered.

The number of drip bags that go onto the stand in a six-hour period was surprisingly more than I thought. Initially, saline solutions and flushes, then the key chemo drugs like Irinotecan, interspersed with drugs like Atropine, Chlorphenamine injected into the cannula and anti-sickness drugs. Some of the anti-sickness drugs injected made my arse feel like I had sat in a load of stingy nettles which again reminded me that moment of the dance of the flaming arseholes on my stag do and being thrown into nettles as a kid! I had to smile.

That first day of chemo was nowhere near as bad as my own long held perception of chemotherapy. I got up from my armchair, felt a bit blurry-eyed for a bit but overall was feeling ready for almost anything relatively quickly. It was me saying to the cancer, if this is proven to be cancer (at that point I didn't know, I still needed the results), that I was at that point in control. If that is all you can throw at me, you need to do better. I felt powerful, another positive.

That evening, the tablet chemo drugs and further anti-sickness drugs became a reality. There were literally boxes of the things, a real cocktail of drugs to take morning and night. These included Ondasetron, Dexamethasone Phosphate, Metoclopramide and the main chemo drug for bowel cancer, Capecitabine. Claudia drew up a matrix of timings for each drug, we didn't want to miss a tablet, ever! It was essential we maximised the dosages to get the complete benefit.

The next day, we casually told the kids, Josh 10, Flynn 13 at the breakfast table, that Daddy wasn't very well. They were disappointed I couldn't go swimming with them! Then, later in the week, whilst on a car journey, Claudia mentioned that it was cancer and there was an audible gasp from the back seat. But Flynn said very matter of factly that he'd learnt about it at school and we all have it inside us and it was just luck if you got it or not! Claudia gave examples of people we knew who'd survived cancer, including my mum who had breast cancer, and they seemed to take it on board that I'd be OK.

The thing for me is that then, at the age of 44, with a perfect home family life, amazing friends, an awesome job with a brilliant team and autonomy, the ability to do what you want pretty much with life, you are suddenly not in control. This process I found myself in, was now in the hands of others. I was learning pretty quickly that in terms of needing to wait for news, this was the norm. Perhaps I was too used to demanding news results with my job, for the biopsy results it was my first experience of accepting the timescales, things in the medical world, frankly, take time. I had to adapt my mind quickly to learn to be patient and wait, I saw it as a new skill to learn a positive addition to my mind/personality. On 5th August, there were still no biopsy results from my liver, it had now been over ten days.

Finally, on 6th August, my oncologist, Dr Jackson, phoned, a serious manner in the tone of his voice. He exchanged polite pleasantries and promptly ended the 11 days of no news. With a professional air which included a few medical words I had never heard of, he gently confirmed that the liver biopsy results were unequivocally cancer spread there from the bowel, the recommended treatment being the chemotherapy which I had already started. Dr Jackson added that the scan results and biopsies would now be sent to the Queen Elizabeth Hospital Birmingham liver team, for further review. I would initially be programmed to receive four chemotherapy sessions. Dr Jackson's view was, that whilst the cancer from the bowel was aggressive to have spread, the liver suggested a middle of the road scenario. It was an unknown trajectory from here on in, we would have to see if it responded to treatment but it was currently inoperable due to the position of the tumours on both sides of the liver. I left the phone conversation looking for the positives and concluded that as no one had said I was terminally ill, in my own perception, I had a chance.

I remember my dear friend, Chloe, coming over with a simple pot of Manuka honey the next day, and giving me a big hug, a tear trickling down her face. Chloe was a nutritionist too, Manuka has proven healing properties, she explained, we all hoped it would fix me. Chloe gave me another hug and I felt positive with the world and what it was throwing at me. I was drawing positive energy, hugs were a good healer.

I needed to talk to people, call it therapy for me, sharing a problem, wearing my heart on my sleeve but it was my way. It is strange phoning family, close friends and giving them the same version of events you have just heard yourself. People react so differently too. Some might, for example, stop, burst into tears, throw up, others are calm collected and rally quickly to rationale, then solid advice. The word cancer, however, stirs up different perceptions, experiences in people's minds as to what it is. Some start writing you off almost as soon as you mention it, others know there may be a chance it can be beaten, a few just don't understand the complexities and how it is pretty much a different case of the disease from person to person. A different stage, a different cell type, where it is, how long it has been there and how aggressive it is, we are all made differently.

With my heart on my sleeve, on 14th August, I posted on Facebook what I was going through and had some amazing messages from people, immediately and over the course of the next few days. For me, it gave me a huge lift, and I could see that a strategy was evolving in the way I was approaching the disease and tackling it.

Chapter 13
Chemo Fun

I never thought I would say it but I started to look forward to my chemo sessions, after all that is the only way in your mind you can approach the experience. I thought of it like a new skill to learn, I imagined it to be like being taken sky diving for the first time, someone there to hold your hand, a bit of fear but you just have to confront those demons and replace them with good vibes. Karen was a great companion, we would chat and sometimes watch box sets on Netflix like *Narcos*, literally watching back-to-back episodes one after the other. Other times, I would be happily working or on a conference call while Karen wrote up my treatment book, carefully logging all my blood results from the previous weekly blood test visit. I often admired how easily and gently the needle would go in, sometimes, I experienced no pain whatsoever. Karen was such a pro!

The thing was, I knew that these sessions with Karen were the bits I needed to maximise to totally benefit from the drugs administered. I needed to do everything I could personally to cooperate, I needed to endure as many of these sessions as I could without complaint. I would attack them with positivity, watching drip after drip of poison filtering down to the cannula and into my veins. Perhaps, I was lucky (I know many suffer with chemo sessions terribly and the side effects can be horrendous) but my mental attitude was faultless and partly due to that, this wasn't anywhere near as bad as I thought it would be, I always looked at it positively. Karen had a lot to do with that mental attitude and the wingmen/pals around me offering regular support.

Yes, I did have the queasiness, diarrhoea, light-headedness, insomnia, loss of appetite, damaged nails, cuts on my feet, loss of taste and hair loss but mind over matter is key.

Sometimes, after a session, I would have something planned regardless of what side effects I would be experiencing. On one occasion, getting a fellow Director Chet to pick me up from the house and take me the 50 miles to work, blurry-eyed just so I could attend the office Christmas fancy dress party. I was so looking forward to seeing some people. We met up with some other guys from the office, me dressed as Top Gun, he as Captain America in an all-in-one-piece leotard-style outfit. I pondered on the trip into work how he would go to the loo, he might need a catheter in a costume like that—it was an American-themed party.

I drank Becks Blue all night but had a great time, having a boogy on the dance floor and getting loads of positive messages and hugs from people. I even got propositioned by a receptionist from the building we occupied, she was drunk and I was stone cold sober, so I told her, due to my treatment, I could potentially shit myself at any time and she soon got the message. Her approach gave me confidence, though, especially with hair falling out everywhere, I certainly didn't feel my best and she was a great looking lady. I smiled as I thought to myself, I really could back fire at any time with the concoction of chemo and antibody drugs from earlier in the day, swimming around me at the point. I just hoped if it did happen, it was a song with an appropriate name, as I imagined people as they evacuated the dance floor, they would look back and hopefully, see the funny side, as 'Grenade' by Bruno Mars perhaps or 'Wrecking Ball' Miley Cyrus blasted out of the speakers.

Trying to sleep after the chemo infusion at the start of a cycle was near on impossible, I felt like I was wide awake through the effect of the steroids, I felt punchy, alert with not an ounce of tiredness. Usually, three days later in the cycle by the Monday, I would sometimes then come down from the steroid effect and start to feel lethargic but overall, I was coping well, carrying on as normally as possible. Over the course of my drug treatment programme, I would eventually endure 16 sessions of chemo by infusion into the blood stream and orally in tablet form, 12 of these sessions had the addition of Cetuximab (the antibody drug) between July 2016 and April 2017.

Cetuximab was not a drug recommended to me by my oncologist. On hearing of my diagnosis from my boss, Jason and

83

prompted by Jason to do so, a fellow colleague, Carl, from our London office had been kind enough to relay a story about his dad's pal's experience being very similar to mine and that an antibody drug had turned around his fortunes. Carl suggested I raise it with my oncologist. It was a piece of advice I took on board and asked my oncologist about it. 'Yes, this might work for you' was the response...

I ended up thinking, 'Well, why the fuck am I raising this with you and not you with me'. I felt pissed off but overall, chuffed to bits there was another weapon in my fight against the disease.

I remembered the day the Cetuximab arrived, it had been delivered by courier to Karen's house, very early in the morning, it was only my third session of chemo. Karen brought the new delivery with the other drugs to my scheduled chemo session that day but looked carefully at the new product and refrigerated bag of liquid and looked concerned.

"I can't give you this here, not in the middle of nowhere (the countryside), you could have an anaphylactic shock and even for me that would be difficult to cope with on my own!" she looked serious and said, "This drug, I really can't give you today, you need the first two administrations in hospital in case you react!"

I was gutted, a delay meant we weren't maximising the chances. I understood that this wasn't down to Karen or the courier, the oncologist was prescribing the drug and should have known this. I wanted everyone around me to be proactive and this guy hadn't spotted this, I was annoyed. I, however, channelled the anger and sought positive focusing on the fact I was still getting my chemo drugs.

It was, therefore, the case, that session four and five of my treatment cycles were given at Cheltenham Hospital, in order that I could be administered the antibody drug under supervision just in case I reacted. For some reason, every time we set out for Cheltenham by car from Hereford early enough to get there on time, leaving at 7:00 a.m. with an eta of 9:00 a.m., the roads were either blocked or diversions made travel slow and stressful for both me and my dad, (my chauffeur). It was as if something was trying desperately to prevent us from getting there by all means.

That stress soon dissipated on arrival, the nurses in the hospital suite were absolutely superb, so nice and friendly it made it so much easier. It was a bit nerve racking having the new drug for the first time, would I react, suddenly start shaking or vomiting or foaming at the mouth? I didn't need to worry, I was fine. Also, as I was now in a hospital, the drugs were given over three hours, not the usual six hours I usually accepted as the norm at home, given that Karen was on her own and needed to be more careful in case I did react. When I did go to Cheltenham on those occasions, Dr Jackson, my oncologist, would stick his head around the door to make sure I was on track with treatment. Again, I would try and carry on as normal. I got my dad to run me from the hospital and drop me the short distance away at Cheltenham train station, this was immediately after my new mix of infused drugs and I caught the train straight into work.

In my wallet, I now carried a chemotherapy alert card. It had a chemotherapy helpline number at the bottom and inside told someone what to do if I experienced a temperature above 37.5 or below 36.0, felt shivery or flu like or generally unwell. If I had a sore mouth or throat, or had persistent diarrhoea to phone immediately. The complications of chemotherapy are potentially life threatening it said, they include Neutropenic Sepsis. I ignored it, I also humorously thought that if I was slumped at my desk at work, it would perhaps be days before someone noticed I had been unconscious and subsequently died. The thing is, as I got on with chemo sessions, I could see the effect on my blood, gradual improvements in scores for different blood characteristics and I had faith in the nutritionist I had now employed having boosted my immune system, I could see these benefits in my blood, I felt confident to travel.

Chapter 14
Changes in the Garden

After absorbing pretty full on news that all is not well with the mothership i.e. me in terms of health, I found myself thrust into a process where I had no control. A medical machine was now in action, the well-oiled wheels and cogs grinding steadily faster around me, chemo nurses, blood nurses, check-up nurses, consultant appointments etc. and everyone around me also adjusting to the reality, their thoughts on outcomes and prognosis forming. People adjust their behaviour even when I was putting a positive face on things. Manly mates, asking to see me with more staring a nature in their faces and the odd tear, others kicking into overdrive trying to speak to me more frequently than they ever had done in the past. Others acknowledging, accepting their view of it and outcome and moving on, hardly to be heard of again. I learnt quickly the massive variance in reactions and with all the medical processes, it is a massively varying wave hurtling towards the shoreline that it is difficult to stay on top of. It was imperative that I did and focused on regularity, normality and getting on with life around this whole new set of systems and necessary changes all programmed to try and save my life.

One autumn evening, during this process, Digger had asked to come to our home and see me, he was one person who had pretty much looked to speak to me every day to see how I was doing since my diagnosis. This was a guy who I had nearly killed three times, prepared to do absolutely anything in his power to help me, even save me. My main interactions with people had, apart from a few, been over text, Facebook, WhatsApp and the phone. Visitors to the house, I was more selective over. I didn't really have time to think about this one, by the time I had said yes, Digger was stood in my kitchen drinking a mug of tea chatting to Claudia about the family, work, usual chitchat. I looked at the visit positively, this was good it would surely take my mind off things, helped me vent what was going on in my head, ultimately a huge positive for which I was very thankful for. I was also intrigued as to why Digger was so eager to come over.

As a businessman, Digger was hugely successful building a number of different companies within a strong business group, each company benefitting from the well-thought out shared infrastructures like supply chain, call centres and systems. Digger was a primary shareholder and doing very well personally. I ventured from my armchair in the lounge when I heard Digger in the kitchen and joined the conversation, we stood in the kitchen talking for a while about the latest run on blood or chemo infusions. Standing and chatting wasn't always easy for me, zapping vital energy and I was conscious of this as we talked but Digger then quickly came around to the point he wanted to discuss.

"Look," he gestured handing me a brochure, "we have just bought a large percentage of the UK shed market and they have bespoke designs for all sorts of garden buildings. Given what hell you have been going through, I have spoken to the MD of the shed company and agreed that we will build a mancave for you of any design you want in your garden, we will build it wherever you want it." I was instantly amazed and of course, refused this fantastic gesture, it was far too generous. Digger, however, threatened to build one anyway if I didn't agree, while I slept one night. I eventually conceded but stressed I wouldn't be much use. "All you have to do is choose the design, we will kit out the inside for you too and you decide what colours you want etc.," he smiled, "this will transform your garden!"

Digger left me with brochures and instructions to choose a design, size, floor, colour and furniture to go in it. Digger was on the phone that evening checking if I was looking into this and kept chasing me. I had a lot of other things on my mind: work issues, the various parts of the medical process and of course, the big one—the unknown, so it wasn't top of my list. However, after a few days of Digger phoning me, I had opted for a 4x5 metre garden room with full-height glazing and glazed doors to the front elevation and one full height glazed window to the side elevation. I opted for a chestnut wooden-effect style floor, cream walls and forest green exterior. Internally, the furniture would be mostly black, the leather sofa bed, glass table and chairs and sideboard all black. The stand-alone statement items would be a SMEG fridge in Union Jack colours, a wall mounted TV, music system and karaoke machine. In the corner would be a cream leather recliner with matching footstool and outside a rattan L-shaped seating area with small table and a huge oval fire pit. All of this choosing and envisaging how the structure would look like before it was built, took my mind off the obvious and was a new and welcome positive focus.

It wasn't long after confirming my design before Digger's work force leapt into action, Digger personally leading the way riding one of his diggers and then yielding a mighty chain saw to clear trees where we had opted to locate the new structure. Digger worked like an animal, some days 7 a.m. to 8 p.m., I occasionally would venture out to see the progress often accompanied by a lunchtime visitor from work, in the process of taking me to a local pub for lunch. I admired the work in progress just before we left. I felt a bit guilty about going off for good food, seeing Digger working so hard but at the back of my mind was conservation of energy levels.

At one point, Digger and his brother Brad toiled for hours to dig out the root bowls of trees in order to create a space for the foundations. The foundations themselves and patio to be created in front of the mancave took a lot of effort, cement needed to be mixed next to the area in question, it was too far from the road for a lorry load of fresh cement. As well as the trees that had been removed we needed to chop down and chip 30 metres of hedges forming part of the garden. On this occasion, I worked with them helping thread branches into the chipper and then helping grout the newly formed patio. I was tiring more easily but the focus was so important. It, however, did wipe me out energy wise for a day or two, I was learning my limits and effect of the chemo on my body and capabilities.

After the cement had set solid, a lorry arrived with flat packs of the garden room and the four-man crew who jumped out of the truck had the structure fully erected and installed with the lights positioned ready for an electrician to attend. Even unpainted, the structure looked awesome, transforming the garden. Digger had been right with his prediction and I felt proud, honoured to be benefitting from such a building.

Digger, however, wanted me to paint it and kept asking how far we had got with the task. Again, I found myself juggling more pressing issues and as I soon found out painting it was a lot harder than I thought and totally exhausting. It took ages to get one coat on and it needed several coats of paint internally and externally. I was completely exhausted doing it but kept pushing myself forward with assistance from Claudia, my dad, Fred and Chloe. Furniture started to accumulate in the garage in flat packs and the electrician attended a number of times to get the lighting working. Things were coming together.

It was late September, when it was completed externally, internally and nestled in its setting amongst the tall trees. A magical moment to see the finished, painted mancave, fully kitted out with furniture. I had ordered canvas prints of special people in my life and these started to populate the walls, along with a Bristol Polytechnic sign retrieved from a skip just before the Poly changed to UWE back in 1991. I ensured I had a couple of Digger who I would always admire and be thankful to for delivering such an awesome project and place for me to retreat to.

Digger had been instrumental in giving me a focus for a number of weeks and I was thankful for the effort and cost that had gone into delivering this fantastic building to me. It was, therefore, appropriate that I named it in honour of Digger's efforts and so after recalling the time I nearly killed Digger with a roll of wall paper, 'The Anaglypta Club' was born. I contacted a local signage company, designed a logo and had a brass sign with 'The Anaglypta Club' and my designed logo screwed above the mancave doors. I can safely say, with its wall-mounted TV, karaoke machine and Bosch speakers, the mancave was crying out, 'this would be a great place for a party'.

In October, I erected, with the help of neighbours and family, the 10 x 5 metre marquee I had bought for my mum's 70th a few years ago, right in front of The Anaglypta Club, leaving just the small patio area between the two structures. We fitted fairy lights inside the marquee along with a red diesel heat blower as it was expected to be cold. I bought a barrel of Butty Bach (Hereford's finest export) and organised a party for close friends who had been there for me so far in the process. At this stage, I literally had no idea if my treatment was working or if I would survive my illness but I felt positive, I had not yet received my first scan results scheduled to be received the day before the party.

On the Friday, the day before the party, I received the news I had been waiting for from the oncologist, that there had been a marked reduction overall in the tumours in my liver, circa 50%. Now this news, despite not being able to drink, was a reason to fully embrace the mancave and christen it as the Anaglypta Club. The party was a go! People travelled to be there and were up for a great night. There was plenty of raw emotion, I was being hugged by loads of people; these were friends who wanted to be there for me. Despite the temperature, some slept in their cars, the paddock leading down to The Anaglypta Club strewn with 4x4s. Karaoke carried on until 4 a.m., I even got a score from the karaoke machine of 99 out of 100 for singing a duet with a mate from university, Bee Gees – Staying Alive. Perhaps this was a message, that, indeed, I was going to stick two fingers up to cancer, stay positive and Stay Alive.

There were plenty of sore heads in the morning, surprisingly, especially the women, they had hit the Prosecco mixed with Limoncello hard joining in my joy.

The party gave me a boost as to who I still was and a positive vibe to not change and allow cancer to control me, I would be very much in control here and carry on as normal. This was the way to realise a milestone in cancer recovery, party hard. I didn't care that my hair was falling out, or that I hadn't been drinking.

It was the lift I needed at that moment almost to say, 'Right, stage 1 of the fight done 1–0 to me, onto stage 2'. I knew I had a long road ahead of me and would have to continue to be patient with the medical process but whilst I didn't know how this might end, I had a feeling of immense positivity from the blood and CT scan results.

Chapter 15
The Business Approach

Most of us lead our lives day to day oblivious to some of life's harder issues and realities. Getting diagnosed with a serious illness is one of those circumstances albeit a bereavement of someone close to you, divorce or financial difficulties are realities but not something everyone experiences. I was one of those before my diagnosis very much taking life for granted, happily leading my ideal life, without too much regard for what could happen to me or what is around the next corner.

To receive any kind of major news, such as you now have a stage 4 cancer and it's spread to your liver and is inoperable, is something that focuses your mind and throws a lot of the crap you were focusing on, out of the window. My mind was racing to block negative thoughts associated with the illness, like deterioration of health, ultimately dying early and leaving people you love behind. I couldn't let those thoughts into my mind. I had to attack this and develop an immediate strategy to fight the disease head on. I set about it as I would deal with a complex issue at work, in business, establishing the circumstances and facts and the best options available to me that were out there following research and recommendations, then developing a master plan, a plan of attack.

I had been open with everyone about being diagnosed and as a result, received a generous helping of mixed advice from every man and his dog but what was I to expect following my public announcement on Facebook? Some of the advice was good advice based on people's experience, some which was well meant but loosely based on hearsay or a general thinking based on what they understood cancer to be.

Engaging my own attitude to do something about circumstances, I quickly muddled through the different aspects of advice and developed a six-point plan:

1) Positivity – remain resolute in my positivity and channel it mentally and physically
2) Diet – get the best possible advice, maintain a strict cancer beating diet
3) Medical – maximise the medical treatment and options and do as much as possible to receive the best available treatment
4) Focus – maintain normal life as much as possible ensuring my focus was on work, outside of work projects, family and friends
5) Avoidance – avoid things which could negatively impact on me mentally or damage me physically
6) Educate – get to understand the detail and specifics such as blood results.

The key of all of these points would be positivity, a strong mental approach, without it, the rest would not get the 100% attention they required. I needed to give myself the best possible chance, with a structured business-like approach, the only problem was I knew very little about cancer, I would need to learn fast. I had always selfishly regarded it as someone else's illness. For all intent and purpose, I was now fighting for my life so the approach needed to be perfect, polished and well supported.

I looked back on my life experiences, for some reason, the high-jinx, risk moments started to come back to me, the linking arms over a car roof at high speed, numerous car crashes and those times I had almost killed people like Digger. The time I had nearly drowned doing practice water rescue drills, when the rope had tangled around my leg in a thunderous weir. I/We had all survived through laughter, instinct, positivity and a good share of luck. I needed to do the same here, I needed to channel that survival instinct roll the right way as I had done in the weir.

I would also draw down on the support network around me, draw positivity from others, unlock those parts of the brain and adapt to the situation. If the situation got worse, I would adapt again and again. I was sure this was in my DNA if it wasn't, I would make it part of me.

This was me, the untamed Maverick living on the edge now needing to confront an even bigger risk. Surely, this was what I wanted? I loved risk? And here it was, the biggest risk of all, my odds were poor and the chances stacked against me but I would be ready for it with total effort.

Those organisational skills from my childhood 'Gangster' days would come into play. I wanted positivity around me, people who cared and who, themselves, wanted to be there and I wanted them to be there. I treasured those positive relationships, very much like it used to be with the friendly homely culture of Wales growing up.

I mentioned earlier in this book that my friend Nina was keen to suggest I got in touch with a nutritionist who had helped her, through diet, with serious illness and that her recommended contact had a fellowship in cancer care and had worked with oncologists in the States where oncology and diet were closer than in the UK. Nina did stress that the nutritionist was in high-demand and difficult to get hold of but this would turn out to be a seriously great recommendation and after diagnosis, I was keen to follow it up as I had read a lot about diet helping illnesses of various kinds.

I was already undergoing chemotherapy, a lot of the medical treatment was a case of administering various drugs either by infusion or tablet at specific times. We would, therefore, require a planner to ensure I fully benefitted, it was obvious it could get confusing as there were so many tablets to take. Amazingly, my chemo nurse was telling me that some patients forget to take the tablets on time or at all and whilst I could see this was potentially very confusing given the number of tablets, I would be maximising the effect of the drugs by being bang on time with the correct dosage and every time.

I had told my boss, Jason, about my diagnosis but overall, not many colleagues knew at that stage. I was, of course, absent from the director's meeting when Jason announced the severity of my illness to a shocked audience, a short period of silence ensued as my fellow directors absorbed the gravity of the news. One guy called Carl broke the silence, saying positively that his dad's friend had survived bowel cancer which had spread to the liver by going onto an antibody drug. Jason immediately asked him to contact me about it. Carl duly did email me details of the drug promptly after the meeting had concluded, highlighting that it wasn't widely available to most patients and that I should suggest it to my Oncologist. I was keen to follow this up, whilst it only worked in the case of some patients due to cell type.

Jason told me that that particular day had been the worst in his professional career. After the meeting, he boarded a train and headed the 100 miles to my office where my team were based, he gathered them together in a boardroom and told them the news. Quite a few were crying, sobs breaking the stoney silence of the room.

Initially, when I was diagnosed, my colleagues at work started to make decisions around me, essentially planning for business continuity given their expectations of how cancer treatment works and that many people take the opportunity to take time out of the business. They expected me to do the same. However, I was keen to have work as a focus and despite the huge list of side effects like the risk of infection, sepsis, chronic vomiting or diarrhoea, I wanted to stay in control and demonstrate, through my stamina, I was capable of functioning as normal. It would take some adjusting but I wanted to challenge myself to do it, not let the cancer get one up on me. I needed projects to focus on outside of work too, I didn't want to end up bored not working and sitting at home trawling the internet which had so many negative cancer stories.

It was things like the negativity on the internet surrounding cancer which I became aware of quite quickly, I was keen to avoid it and avoid anyone that I didn't get a positive vibe from. I would learn some people reacted as expected, some truly stepped way above expectations and others didn't react as expected, hardly getting involved or commenting at all. That said, people have their lives to live and I totally got that but it was almost the fact once they knew you were diagnosed with a serious illness, they had already written you off. This included family and friends but a small minority. I would simply avoid them.

I needed to get a lot closer to the specifics of the illness. I had learnt already that the regular blood test I was having, split my blood into a large number of categories, measuring my immune system through things like white blood cells and platelets and how cancer proteins were measured circulating in the blood stream. If I could have an impact on these regular data through positive actions and diet, medicine then it could only be a positive.

Chapter 16
The Treadmill

I started to fall into a routine, chemo became part of my life along with the regular blood tests, consultations, tablets and scans. I made the disease fit around me not the other way around and I tried to manage my expectations, knowing in my mind what to expect if a treatment was due. I would imagine it before it happened and this helped when it actually did occur, it was pretty much as expected. I would always set something to look forward to post treatment.

The waiting for things to happen is hard with all things medical. I was either waiting for blood test results, taking a keen interest, waiting for scan results or waiting for the consultant to return my calls. You learn to be patient as a patient, the medical machine is effective but it can be slow but we have to take on board people are doing their jobs. Time started to fly by. Each week, there was something happening, a needle being stuck in me or something involving a doctor's surgery room or home visit by the homecare nurses. I measured time in the number of chemo sessions, it felt like I was on a treadmill which never ended, I was part of a huge process, when one session ended after only a few days break another one would start.

I was concentrating so hard on things like diet and doing everything possible from my end, this helped time fly by also but I needed to know whether any of the process was helping. My main regular update was from Karen, who when turning up to administer the chemo intravenously, would fill out my chemo book with my blood results after she had wired me up. This would list all my blood results from the blood test a few days earlier. I started to look forward to chemo sessions because of this moment, it helped me ignore the needles.

"So, Karen," I would ask with hope in my voice, "what are my bloods doing today?"

From day one, I could see the improvements in key elements of my bloods either rising for the good or falling for the good depending on which they were. The key yard markers for me were my immune markers such as white blood cell count (WCC), neutrophils (NEUT) and my CEA score (tumour marker). It filled me with confidence to see the white blood cell count rising and the CEA score falling, it made me feel like all the effort and my strategy was working. Every session now being at two weekly intervals, I would eagerly await the blood test results, sat there in my armchair, hoping Karen had good news.

A pattern started to emerge, each session, my bloods were showing good results, I really hoped this would result in reductions in the size of the tumours on the scan results, that really would be something to celebrate.

That first CT scan before the party, for example, was scheduled for October 2016, I had been more apprehensive for enduring that scan and anticipating what the results might be, than anything in the process so far. For me, this was a critical moment in the process. If the tumours were actually getting bigger, despite all the effort, I was effectively dying albeit I was perhaps slowing the process. If, on the other hand, they were seen to be shrinking, I was winning at least controlling the process in some way, if the latter, this would be falling in line with the blood results to date. Loads of things go through your mind such as, if I am dying it might not be far off and what is death, what is it like, I am not ready for it, or am I?

I remember going into the scanner, determined to give the best scan possible lying as still as possible, to give them the clearest picture possible. The waiting for the results for this one would be the hardest and I wasn't wrong. It takes time, whole teams need to review the scan before they will tell you anything. A few days went by, then a week, I was really anxious to know and I chased my oncologist's secretary each day by phone, despite her being the loveliest person, there was little she could tell me.

That scan result news that came on the Friday before the party which was nearly ten days after I had had the scan. Those words, 'there has been a marked reduction, 50% reduction' resonated around my brain. The immediate message I computed in my mind was quite simply the strategy was working, I was overjoyed for the first time since being diagnosed, I was now telling myself I can beat this. In my mind, there were now things I wanted to do more long-term, if I was able to beat this, I so looked forward to the day I might win the battle and beyond.

Chapter 17
The Flood

My chemo sessions were typically on a Thursday every three weeks and then once Cetuximab had been added to the cocktail of intravenous drugs, it became fortnightly sessions being wired up with tablets for nine days between with four days off. Whilst I felt a bit blurry-eyed immediately after a session, I was maintaining my routine of getting up at 5:30 a.m., being showered, changed and downstairs by 6:30 a.m. and leaving the house for work by car at 7:00 a.m. On average, my commute to Birmingham was about one and a half hours, approximately 50 miles.

It was important for me to take the tablets, the main one being Capecitabine circa 2000mg in the morning and then another 2000mg at night at precisely the right intervals. This was all part of the strategy to maximise the benefit of the medicine, try and hit the recommended intervals exactly on time. This, in reality, meant leaving the house with my tablets in a wooden egg cup covered in cling film and a bacon sandwich wrapped in foil, with a bottle of water in the car cup holder. This meant that, en route, I could take the four large tablets 20 minutes after eating the sandwich. Bacon was not on my nutritionists recommended list, but you have to have some vices and 'boy', did I need it that day!

On this particular morning, it was wet and had rained continuously for a few days. The route I could take to work was one of four, two backcountry routes via Bromyard, one via Worcester and the other via Ledbury and the motorway networks. This particular morning, I had chosen one of the Bromyard routes and one which took me to a small village called Knightwick, where a turn off the main Bromyard-Worcester road would take me up a steep hill called Ankerdine and further into Worcestershire. I knew Knightwick well, it was where I had completed a large part of my swift-water rescue training on the thunderous man-made weir on the River Teme just below the road bridge. The River Teme was a scary river, narrow and tree lined, fast flowing in places and prone to bursting its banks with the extra water volume during downpours, the water from the welsh mountains finding its way down a few days later to the lower land counties like Worcestershire.

My training on the weir had given me a different respect for the river, its sheer power, complex hydrology and deafening roar as it cascaded the weir. People die on weirs, as you approach the weir the water speeds up until you hit downward ramp, almost like a slide which spans the width of the river. At the bottom of the slide is a large wave of white water which hits you like being thrown into a washing machine even if you are wearing the latest high tech safety gear and personal floatation device. The speed of the water and bubbling cauldron sucks you downwards and along past the wave and spits you out downstream towards another wave feature some 15 metres back. This second wave will suck people down under and then the current pulls you back up stream towards the first wave at the point of the weir, by this time you are completely underwater.

It becomes a vicious circle of being dragged along the bottom thrown to the top and battered as you drown against the man-made concrete structure. Even as potential rescuers, we were told by our instructors there were big risks training on this river and the weir. We were using hand signals as hearing speech was impossible. We spent days on the weir simulating rescues, doing tethered swims and putting safety lines across the weir at diagonals to catch the casualty and steer them to the bank. As I slowed the car to turn off the Worcester Road, there was the weir, I glanced at its ferocious appearance, it was like driving past a pride of lions, that needs to be kept at a distance and commanded respect.

On this particular morning, as I drove my BMW 330d into Knightwick, I thought back to the river and knew instinctively as I turned onto the parallel road, it would be in flood. It was so high at the point where it meandered past the bank adjacent to the Talbot public house that it had over-spilled, flooding the road in front of the pub right at the bottom of Ankerdine hill, the route I was on. The river just 200 metres or so above the weir was now indistinguishable from the tarmac and I was slowing to a halt watching nervous drivers ahead of me and coming towards me negotiate this hazard, trying to second guess where the road actually was. Some parts seemed more shallow than others and most vehicles were getting across, making waves but were succeeding.

One trick seemed to be to drive into the pub car park near the river then turn out of the entrance of the car park nearest the pub into the floodwater and out onto the tarmac as it rose upwards up Ankerdine. It was the shortest section of water. It was my turn, so I went for it and immediately wished I had brought the X-Trail, my trusted 4x4. Even though my BMW had xDrive, effectively 4x4 capability, the trouble with my sporty 330d was that the air intake was so very low on the front of the car, below the front lights. As the water seemed to make waves at the corners of my bonnet, a light came on the dashboard, the car lost power and failed. I had tried to keep acceleration high, to keep water blowing out of the exhaust, the problem was this had ensured more water was being sucked in through the air intakes. I was literally stranded in the middle of the lake of water around me. The car would not restart.

Furthermore and annoyingly, vehicles continued to try the crossing around me, people eager to continue with their daily routines, determined to overcome this obstacle. Each time a vehicle tried the crossing, my car would get hit by the wake, a series of waves hitting the side of my car, a noisy sudden slapping sound of water thrown against the metal panels of my vehicle. I was embarrassed, me a trained rescuer the only car to get stranded here. I got funny looks constantly, toots and a few cheeky comments from the cock-sure drivers in their land rovers proud to be finally putting their expensive bits of kit to proper use other than the school run. I couldn't get out of my car, without wading up to my waist, so I phoned another rescuer organisation, the AA.

It was a Hamlet cigar moment, as I sat there, helplessly thinking I had probably written off my engine but I didn't really care. With the illness I had, there were bigger, more important things in life than cars to worry about. With that, I opened my tin foil sandwich and had my breakfast, it was time for my routine of food followed by my Capecitabine tablets. The looks I got were priceless, there was a guy sat in his car in the middle of a flooded road, stranded but seemingly oblivious, eating his breakfast.

I was lucky the AA man arrived within 20 minutes and somehow got me nearer the edge of the floodwater by towing me, I had to communicate to him through my open window. Many attempts to get the engine going failed, it seemed inevitable that the beamer was heading back to the dealer on the back of the lorry. Something inside told me to ask the AA engineer to have one last go, whilst he looked resigned he agreed. This time, the noise was different, the engine was trying to turn and we both heard it. Suddenly, she burst into life and from the open bonnet a jet of water shot from some part of the engine in almost a vertical motion. After a quick test drive up Ankerdine, the saviour Mr AA, told me how lucky I had been and set me on my way. Perhaps I was too blasé about this but this was the reality, I was simply glad I had taken my tablets on time and that this was another step in the right direction against cancer.

Chapter 18
Dealing with Side Effects

Sitting in your mate's kitchen, contemplating having your hair shaved off after never having asked a hairdresser to do it in 44 years is a daunting prospect. It shakes the foundations of your confidence, just the thought of walking into a room of people who you know and them noticing the drastic change in your appearance is a leveller psychologically. However, taking that switch in your mind and flipping it, to confident positivity and this could be a good thing, this could be a great new style. Digger had committed to having his head shaved at the same time as the buzz of the electric hair-trimmer got louder. His other half didn't fuck around, with a sweeping motion (and she could have chosen either one of us sat beside each other in front of her), she drove the trimmer right up and then down his scalp, creating a 8cm parting of shaved hair from back to front. Digger looked shocked and the wry smile from his other half implied she may leave his hair like that. It looked daft but I was next and within an instant, clumps of hair disappeared, falling gently onto the floor around me. I remember looking in the mirror thinking how the baldness and its features reminded me of my dad's side of the family. On the plus side, I had the right shaped head for no hair, no odd lumps albeit my ears looked bigger.

As for Digger, I expected him to be arrested as soon as he set foot outside of the house. With his brace as well, which, at 44, he was being made to wear for at least nine months, most kids would now be very scared. Still, someone had offered to share my pain, to go through the same thing and they didn't have cancer, I wouldn't forget that gesture, it was an admirable trait.

When you find yourself in a system of treatment, a set of unknown processes, many of which might have a negative stigma attached to them, like chemo for example, you can look forward and think how hard can this possibly be? What experience that I have been through in my years on this planet, would this compare to…?

I looked for example at things from the past, like high-jinx moments where I had hurt myself, maybe cut myself, injured myself playing sport, been in hospital in the past or to the doctors for immunisations. I was psychologically, mentally preparing myself for the future. How bad could it all be? I had survived those experiences and felt good when I had emerged from them, I was determined that these would be no different.

I had heard bits about chemo over the years but my understanding was limited and I think I sort of thought it was worse than radiation treatment and meant being wired up to something for a long time. A needle in my arm for a prolonged period, God forbid that didn't sound good.

Mentally, I was seeing this as a challenge, whatever the treatment would be, I would challenge myself to rise above the side effects, come out of it thinking that was nowhere near as bad as I thought it would be! In every instance, this was the case, needles, drugs, tablets, biopsies, operations and any medical side effects.

I saw a needle as a test, to see how tolerant I was to pain, I got so used to needles I looked forward to them (I know that sounds morbid) but the positive thoughts of looking differently in advance of the experience had changed my mental attitude. I was often amazed how good nurses are at their jobs, a slight scratch was often negligible. I learnt how to soak my arms to pump up a vein, keep my arm straight so the needle would slide along the vein easily and help the nurse find a good vein.

The drugs themselves, go in slowly through a cannula, you can feel the toxicity in your blood gradually taking effect. Again, a challenge, in some ways, it was like getting pissed but trying to sober up but to a much lesser extent. I loved the moment the needle came out after six hours being wired up, how did I feel at that moment? I would try desperately to be normal and carry on as usual doing everyday life things. I was coping easily, rising above this.

Side effects for chemo are listed as pretty horrendous, diarrhoea, chronic sickness, lack of energy, hair loss, on top of this, I was on an antibody drug where the side effects were acne, cuts to feet and hands, damage to finger and toe nails, dry skin, no taste. I had a bit of this and that but I would wake up and think I am not going to let this beat me. Some side effects were hard especially the ones where they impact your confidence, like acne at the age of 44 or hair loss, cracked nails.

You know what though, you just get on with things, this is a temporary thing and it's something new to break up your day. I know that sounds weird too but I looked forward to losing my hair so I could try going bald, I had never done it. With acne, I wanted to know what it was like, I had a teenage son who was going through it, a perfect way to learn how I could support him. Again, a positive outlook on something not immediately apparent as having any side effects. Acne was hard though, try walking into your office with puss filled spots on your cheeks and forehead, some would occasionally burst in meetings, I would notice blood or puss suddenly on my hand, perhaps a fingernail accidentally scuffing the surface.

The combination of drugs, seemed to affect my urination, I even had acne on my todger too, stomach and arms. I ended up on antibiotics 100mg a day to combat the acne caused by the Cetuximab as with spots on the end of your knob it is hard to piss straight. Still, look at the positive, it wasn't going to be for long and I would appreciate my body more when I was free of the spots and acne.

The hardest side effect had to be my feet. The long vertical and horizontal paper like cuts needed inspecting by nurses when they did my check-ups for infection. I didn't mind them but if I walked even slightly too far, I would be punished unable to walk even short distances as a result, the pain being a lot. It made me appreciate my feet more, all that hockey and running, I swore I would do more of that once I was off these drugs and these drugs were doing a good job apparently, if my side effects were this bad.

Another side effect was my teeth. I was told by the oncologist and it repeated it in the leaflets that any dentistry visits should be put on hold until after the chemo treatment. All I knew was a noticeable deterioration in the colour around the edge of my teeth, like a brown stain that looked permanent and wouldn't come off. I tried brushing extra hard but even that didn't work and was advised against. I desperately needed a scale and polish but I would have to wait it out. On occasion, I tried the small Yshaped flossing wires between my teeth and actually saw small flakes of brittle tooth enamel come off as I did so. Again, it was a short-term pain for long-term gain, I would see a dentist at some point in the future and I thought, why not then just get your teeth whitened Beavan!

With things like biopsies, camera surveys of your back passage (flexible sigmoidoscopy), I would have something to look forward to afterwards. I remember after having my liver biopsies in day surgery I was sitting with my mate Liam and his wife Nina a few hours later, having a herbal tea.

With results, regardless of what they would be, I often organised a social to occur just after receiving them, one being the christening of the mancave. It was a great feeling to see people who cared for you and wanted to be part of your recovery.

The operations were easier than I thought. OK, so you have blood tests and cannulas pre-op, inserted in your body but it is through such good nurses and doctors who literally make it as painless as possible, in some ways going to hospital was like a mini holiday, different interesting and part of life's rich tapestry.

I could look back at any point in this process and say, 'look what I have coped with already...yeah, I am kicking some ass, loads of needles a massive scar, loads of poisonous drugs, hair loss, acne, biopsies, regular blood tests...' but you can get through it and know that you challenged yourself to rise above these tests of character and gave it your best shot. Be a warrior and be a lion ready to fight another day. I know that somewhere inside us, we all have that capability if we channel into it. I am a stronger person having been through these side effects and know I could cope with a lot more, you will have to drag me off this planet.

The hardest side effect for me was, by far, giving up beers or a bottle or two of wine with mates. Whilst nobody told me to give up alcohol, it was another test of character for me. Could I do it? Would I feel better for it? My immune would certainly be stronger in my view. Becks Blue became my alternative drink, no alcohol but tasted very similar to the real thing. It is another positive, I will keep after this process, albeit I don't feel better for giving up booze, I was never an alcoholic and I would go back to it once I felt ready.

There will be more side effects ahead, they interest me, none scar me, throw what you want at me Mr Cancer, I really will beat you running toe to toe with you for as long as I can, either give up or learn I am strong in the face of your sneaky stealth.

Chapter 19
The Tide Is Turning

I was sat working on my laptop, a Monday morning 6th March. It was a bright sunny day, a strong show that spring was here after the gloomy wet weather there had been recently. I had opted to have a calmer week, the previous week had been manic going into the office every day and London to a directors meeting on Thursday, I had felt a bit under the weather, a bit whacked, I was determined this week would be easier.

Where I would sit to work, was at the dining room table with large almost floor to ceiling windows to my right, giving a view to the stone well, lawns and trees. To my left, another window looking out onto the rear of the house and hawthorn hedge. I had watched a small wood mouse (of which there were plenty), traversing across the bare hedge, weaving between the twigs and thorns at least two metres off the ground. Wood mice had proved a nuisance getting into the attic of the house, I had caught several over the time we lived here. The most beautiful of creatures, a ginger/brown coat with a white under belly but set on eating anything including your electrics.

As I had taken a break from working and moved towards the kitchen to put the kettle on, my personal mobile had gone off to the tune of *Wild Wild West* by Will Smith. I could see, from the name displayed on the Samsung S7 Edge, it was my oncologist, Tom Jackson. The name on the screen often filled me with apprehension, this was the guy who had delivered very frank news in the past and could literally change your life with a phone call. I hesitated listening to the ring get louder and then opted to answer it before it reverted to answer machine.

We politely exchanged civilities, Tom had spotted it was my birthday the next day and wished me a good birthday and asked me how I was doing? I imagined Tom sat at his desk, my medical profile filling his laptop screen. I explained I was fine and that even some of the side effects were nowhere near as bad as they had been, they could be but I was always keen to not let them get to me. We discussed the painful sliced cuts on my feet and my raging acne, which Tom had prescribed 100mg antibiotics for daily—Doxycycline.

Tom then moved onto the main reason for his call, "I have just heard from the QE (Queen Elizabeth Hospital)," he took a measured long breath inwards, "they want to see you, which is great news!"

…I was suddenly so excited and shocked at the same time, having waited since July 2016 for even the slightest sign from the liver experts based at the QE, that they could do anything. Tom continued with positivity in his voice, "I think this is a good sign, it means they must think they can do something for you and will contact you directly to arrange to see you, I imagine they will want to do a more detailed liver MRI scan." Tom said he was pleased for me and after a brief chat left me to think this massive news through.

I have to say, I was really chuffed, whilst my cancer cells/tumours had reduced with the chemo and antibody drug, the key aim for me was to get them out of my body, cancer cells being clever and adaptable, learning how to spread. I phoned and texted a few people to get a positivity hit and I knew these were people who would want to know and cared.

Sure enough, I had received an appointment to go and finally meet a liver specialist on 17th March. The QE was one of the leading hospitals in the world, military casualties from recent conflicts such as Afghanistan were flown there for surgery and it had some of the top consultants in their field based there.

The day before the appointment, I had arranged to meet Larry in my lunch break for a couple of chilled Becks Blues. Larry was chipper, brimming with smiles and laughter. Enquiring about his general, well-being Larry retorted that he had seen four pussies in one week and had one blowjob after meeting a colleague for a coffee, walking her to her car and managing to impress on her the need for a kiss and a cuddle. It took my mind off things, it still puzzled me how this guy, who desperately sought the love of a female, had no problem in getting what a lot of men strived for, regular, uncomplicated, interesting shagging without much effort. I only hoped he was wearing protection, or half of the Midlands could be sharing each other's health specifics.

I told Larry that I was apprehensive about the meeting coming up with the consultant, I suspected another serious, well-educated expert in his field that had the power to deliver life-changing news or a prognosis on my future in the blink of an eye. As with all my close friends, Larry told me to remain positive and it was likely to be good news given the oncologist's comments a few days earlier. I was positive but quietly nervous, I had waited ten months to see the liver unit at the QE and now, it was happening quickly.

The 17th had come all too soon and I had arranged to meet my wife, Claudia, at the QE half an hour prior to the appointment. The QE was a young hospital and an imposing building almost alien in appearance with three gigantic large oval linked structures with sloping rooflines dominating the surrounding area, towering high above any other buildings. It was relatively easy to park in a multi-storey immediately adjacent to the main entrance and just walk a short distance into the galleried main entrance hall. It was a case of self check-in via barcode scanning from the appointment letter and then sitting and waiting. I had been a private patient until now, with most of my chemo at home, here it was different, I was an NHS patient and the waiting was a lot longer.

Eventually, I was called forward to my meeting, walking past the other 60–70 patients awaiting their various hospital appointments. From what I read on the screen as I walked to the consultant's door, the hospital treated circa 1,800 patients a day, over 15,000 a week. This was some impressive operation.

The consultant was friendly, well-educated, middle-aged and, I gauged, likely of Indian decent. Before he even started to speak, I noticed on his screen behind him, a letter I had accidentally seen before a few months earlier, from my consultant to my GP, stressing how many of these metastases I had in my liver and that surgery was not an option. This made me think I was about to get bad news.

He began quietly by asking me about my treatment so far and whether I had seen the CT scans.

"No," I replied, "I have only been told what they showed," and with that the consultant waved me closer towards his screen.

"We can only see the three tumours now and the good news is they all seem close to the surface of your liver. This makes surgery a lot more straight-forward in terms of liver operations and we anticipate removing no more than 5% of your liver." I was amazed by the comments and as I started to feel more relaxed and relieved he continued, "Your body has responded amazingly to the treatment so far and I want you to come off chemo and all drug treatment now, I think we should be able to schedule you for an operation in about six weeks' time, this won't be a key hole operation due to the position of one of the tumours, so you will have a big scar, in all likelihood, the scar will be down your front and under your ribs."

If I am honest, I didn't like the sound of being cut open to that extent, I felt pretty good, I knew that cutting through skin and muscle would take some time to come around from. The consultant explained that I would be in intensive care for 24 hours, in hospital circa seven days and would take 6–8 weeks to recover from the scar.

I wasn't jumping for joy, yes this was a massive positive but I was in a process and nowhere near the end. I saw this as a competitive event that I had to win and whilst this was perhaps the biggest obstacle I might face, the race was a long one and this wasn't even the halfway point. Some patients don't respond to the chemo in the first place, my body had and I had gone from a non-operational status to operable in nine months. Yes, I would be in the best surgical hands for an operation but even getting through this, by what I understood of the position I was in, I would still need a bowel operation later in the year if I survived the liver operation.

There was also one caveat to the consultants intended course of action for me, an MRI scan which was more detailed than a CT scan and would show if there was anything else evident in my liver. This would be scheduled in the next three weeks, I would then see the consultant again before they pressed the go button.

I left the hospital numb, not knowing what to feel, I was good at adapting but this adaptation needed time. I had to hit this forthcoming new phase of treatment, with all positivity and my mind would have to work fast to get me into the right gear.

The MRI scan was scheduled for a Saturday, in April at 8:00 a.m., again at the QE. My dad had offered to pick me up at 6:00 a.m. to get me there. I hoped it wasn't some warped April fool's joke, if it was, I wouldn't be laughing. When we got to the hospital, it was completely deserted, normally a mass of humans darting in all directions to different medical departments or diving into the smattering of cafes and magazine shops in between visiting relatives or friends. Even the imaging department wasn't open and when, eventually, someone did open the door to the scanning ward, we were the only people sat in a vast waiting room.

I was used to the CT scans which were usually in a truck stationed at the back of the Hereford Private Hospital. It was my least favourite part of the process to date, a fat cannula in your arm to ensure the contrast dye enters your blood stream quickly which sometimes really hurt when the needle went in. The upside was that it was relatively quick in and out of the lorry in about 15 minutes after holding your breath for three separate scans, one of which as you hold your breath as instructed, the dye hits your blood stream at the same time. I had heard the MRI scan was a lot longer and I assumed that would mean another fat needle in my arm for a longer period.

When I eventually got called through from the deserted waiting room, the two nurses were top draw, friendly and experienced. First, the needle and then the plastic tube entered my arm on the opposite side to my elbow inserted gently and professionally by the nurse. I didn't feel it or at all for that matter while I was in the scanner. If you suffer from claustrophobia, an MRI scanner is not for you, it's essentially a tube shape, with a diameter that is not much wider than me lying down with my arms at my side, I don't consider myself too fat either, 5 feet 10 inches and, at the time, about 13 stone!

Once in the scanner, I shut my eyes, they had given me some ear defenders and when the nurses exited to the safety of a side room, I understood why. This machine made hundreds of different noises, alternating noises for each scan. There must have been 20 different scans all in all some I would be asked to hold my breath, some holding your breath as the contrast dye funnelled through my veins. That said, I didn't feel the dye going in, unlike a CT scan where you felt the liquid almost rising across your shoulder and a warm sensation around your groin as though you had swamped in your underpants.

The hardest part of the MRI scan was trying to stay as still as possible for so long while recovering from holding your breath. I was glad to get out but on the whole it was a positive experience. The way to look at it is, you are one step closer to the ultimate goal. I knew I didn't have long to wait for the results, my next appointment with the QE liver team was on 6th April.

Of course, I felt a degree of apprehension before seeing the consultant again, had my MRI scan been OK? Was there something new not evident on the CT scan? It was just a case of waiting and getting the low down.

Going from being in total control of everything in your life to being told to comply with a set of processes and procedures as your best chance of survival, takes some getting used to, the hardest thing to get used to is perhaps the waiting to hear news and critical news, critical news to you that is. Waiting for the results of an MRI scan for six days for some would be unbearable, again you have to look at it positively and train your mind to look at other things, to acknowledge the need to be patient. Sometimes, the waiting was two or three weeks but you have to acknowledge that experts, often teams are discussing your scan on complex matters like surgery and the best route for your particular circumstances. It can be worth the wait and in my case it was.

The day to get my results eventually came in the form of a face meeting with the liver unit. After another long wait in the QE waiting room after checking in again by barcode, the consultant I was seeing was an hour behind schedule according to the screen in the waiting area, eventually after one hour and ten minutes, we were guided into the consultant's room. The nurse who had called us through sat in on the meeting too.

The consultant/registrar was, I would guess, my age circa 45. His first question was, "What is your understanding of what is happening to you in terms of treatment, what have you been told?" I ran through pretty much what I had been told prior to the MRI scan, I'd been told to come off the drugs and that subject to the MRI scan results, I would be having an operation and be in hospital up to a week, intensive care 24 hours. I went into detail, detail that I wasn't going to be forgetting in a hurry given the gravity of the situation. This guy seemed impressed with my summary and jokingly suggested I come and work at the hospital. My mind certainly didn't think that was a good idea, far too serious a job for me, without much down time and too many hours from what I had heard.

"Yes, pretty much correct," the consultant said smiling, "the good news is the MRI scan does not show any further areas and we are still just seeing the three tumours and one cyst. The cyst is nothing to worry about, a large proportion of the adult population have them and it shouldn't cause a problem." He looked at his screen and then gathered some papers and rose to his feet, saying, "Subject to me just checking with the lead surgeon today that he is happy with your scan results, we will book you in to operate, the nurse here will guide you through any questions you have around the operation while I pop out for a few minutes," and with that he left the room.

Most of what the nurse had to say, I already knew but I asked questions anyway determined to double check everything, knowledge was crucial in my view. From her overview, I would be coming in the night before the operation and be put to sleep early in the morning through a cannula. I would be out for the count while they administered an epidural to my spine, a catheter, put a tube down my nose, another cannula in my neck into an artery vein and numerous other medical delights before they even got to the operation and slicing me open with their sharpest scalpel underway. They would then use the world's biggest staple gun to fix me back up, leaving a drain for any nasty blood, puss or bile to come out. The epidural would remain in my spine for three days to numb the pain around the surgical area.

Well, I thought, *this is serious shit, I am going to have to jump through these hoops if I am going to survive.*

Before I knew it, the registrar was back and signing me up, getting me to agree to the above horrors inflicted on my body and to be at their disposal for medical treatment and research. I was now in their hands completely, I had to trust in the process. My operation date, provided there were no liver transplants that suddenly emerged overnight, would be 10th May. A liver transplant from anywhere in the country, would arrive in all likelihood by air ambulance and would be the only thing to take priority over my case and effectively take my place in the queue. The chance of it happening was, however, slim. I left feeling positive I had a definitive date but again, trying to get my mind around being cut open and sliced open in not the too distant future.

Chapter 20
Keeping the Norms

At the age of approximately 15/16, holidays were still periods of boredom for me, an only child and seldom did we go abroad as a family. Fred, one of my closest friends then and now, had come over to hang out and we had ended up walking to Huntington Lane a rural route which looped away from my parent's house from Three Elms road, meandering in a series of pretty postcard type bends to eventually join Kings Acre road and bring you back to their house after a few miles of rural air. Half way along this lane is a stone-block bridge which used to be a railway bridge, the narrow lane being carried over the former railway line. The rail line had been torn up probably in the 60s but the bridge remained built sturdily of rough-cut stone pillars with an iron structure and panels supporting the road works of the lane above.

I would never have suggested climbing one of the massive pillar fascias holding up the lane above, it just wasn't me, I was fearful of heights and we had no safety gear, plus it was a windy day. In essence, however, that day, it was Fred's grand plan to overcome our mutual boredom, we were young men full of testosterone and this would, to him, simply prove our aspiring manhood. I peered over the side of the bridge and tried to dissuade Fred who was set on doing this regardless of me taking part. It seemed so far down to the bottom, I estimated at least 25 metres.

After some discussion, Fred told me to stay on the bridge and act as an extra pair of eyes guiding him to the next hand or foothold and with that, he set off down the lane to climb over the field gate 200 metres away and trudge back across the field at the lower level, to the base of the bridge and the foot of the pillars below me.

Fred was physically stronger than me at that age, he was more rugged and whilst I was a strong runner, he did weights, played rugby and generally was interested in testing his abilities, scaling the bridge being within his mental understanding of what he could achieve.

Fred made it look easy, to be honest, I did assist a bit with spotting good hand holds for him during his ascent but it didn't take him long to reach the top of the pillar and then gently pull himself onto the top of the pillar and haul himself over the metal side panel of the bridge and land beside me. "Your turn…!" he said pushing me down the lane towards the field gate. The wind was picking up.

The idea didn't sit well with me but I was eager to be more physical, like Fred and to prove to myself I could overcome this obstacle. That is all it was in my mind—an obstacle, it would soon be over no matter how difficult. I would confront my fear and not let the pressure or weight of the task get the better of me. I was trying to turn a negative in my brain into a positive. Every part of me was saying no, this is not safe, this is a huge risk, you're shit at climbing, in fact, when had I climbed anything apart from bars and a rope in the gym at school? If I fell, who would I leave my bike to?

I reached the base of the bridge, and stared up at Fred who was peering down at me, smirking. "Come on, you wimp, get stuck in," he yelled down goading me to commence the upward journey. I gulped, nervously…this was peer pressure with bells on it.

Knowing that the more I stayed rooted to the spot, the more I would psych myself out of it, I put my first foot on a stone, grabbed a rock higher up and launched myself into a climb. I learned quickly that there were plenty of handholds but this was hard work on my limbs, heaving the weight of my body up was in itself a challenge, I had never climbed anything vertical. I was fine and going along well with Fred's encouragement and observations assisting my next foot or handholds, but then I looked down. I must have been half way up when I was filled with a terror and dread a dark reality that I could actually fall a long way and get hurt or even die. I pressed myself almost flat into the pillar, almost akin to a child hugging his mother's breast on the first day at nursery not wanting to go or leave the safety of the hug.

The wind had picked up too and here was the reality, trying to go down looked equally as hard as going up. I was weighing the options in my mind, I needed a solution that would lead to my survival, I was too young to throw everything away falling from some disused Herefordshire bridge. I opted to not look down or back and to continue upwards. Every move was terrifying but in some way, gratifying as I neared my ultimate goal. The hardest part was controlling my fear internally, calming my breathing and trying to balance my physical exertions with conserving energy for the next move. I had to remove all negative thoughts from my brain and just keep on going with a clear focus in mind towards the road above. The top of the pillar was terrifying, I had to clamber into a position with my body where I could reach up vertically along the flat vertical metal side of the bridge. There were no handholds here, one false move and I would be falling to where once steam trains clattered along the single-track line and the hard smooth earth below.

With a final effort, I overcame a nightmare and vaulted my body over the metal onto the road, feeling relieved but exhausted. I had been challenged, adapted my mind, focused and overcome a major obstacle. It was a new mental skill and I would use it again in the future. "Well done, mate!" Fred offered as a welcome home greeting.

Once diagnosed with cancer, you can see how for some it is a case of—that is it, it becomes a huge burden and challenge that is insurmountable. It is likely to weigh heavy on the mind, absorb every thought and moment, dominate your mood and life. It will drag you down if this happens and it will start beating you if that happens. That negativity is infectious and impacts those around you too.

On being diagnosed, people around you start to develop their own reactions to the news before you have even had a chance to set a course or adapt, develop a strategy. At work, my senior colleagues were making steps to protect the business before the medical practitioners had commented, anticipating I would be riding this long dark road at home and no longer turning up for the day job. Socially, people anticipate you won't be turning out for supper or get-togethers either. Again, some people diagnosed, will accept this and do as they are told. I am not one of those people.

For me, it would be business as usual. I had been challenged, stopped in my tracks, given a stark piece of news and it was now a major obstacle to me, my life and I didn't even know if it was something possible to overcome. I didn't want to spend hours researching it or scouring the internet for similar stories, I had read an article about an actor formerly in the TV series, the Bill, that had had bowel cancer and it just seemed very negative to me. For me, I simply needed to focus and carry on. So that was my plan.

On reading the side effects of the chemo and other drugs, some maybe inclined to stay indoors. They list the risk of infection, low energy and chronic sickness and diarrhoea and there were a few days where I took it easy near the start but I was keen to establish my parameters, what was my body capable of doing during the treatment? What nutrition did I need to get on with my day-to-day job? What work could I do while wired up to a drip during chemo for six hours every two weeks?

I was lucky in the fact I could work from home but I was running a team at work and wanted to be there. Early in the process, I made a statement that unless told not to, I would be working as normal and whether from home or at work, I intended to carry on. My boss, Jason, was very supportive as were the firm. At this point in the process, I hadn't missed a day of work other than one for my bowel and another for my liver biopsies.

In simple terms, I needed to maintain regular focuses and work was a key one.

Chapter 21
Beyond My Control

The date had arrived for my journey to the Queen Elizabeth Hospital Birmingham, I would have surgery the next day on my liver.

I had organised for my dad to drive my wife and I to the hospital the evening before the op, I would be admitted to a ward on 9th May. Saying goodbye to the kids was tricky, my youngest son (11) was in floods of tears albeit my eldest son (14) was assuming an air of responsibility which I admired. As we exited the drive and onto the farm track, I watched my youngest son, hugging his nan and being shepherded back into the house for consolement, I had to ignore it and focus on the road ahead, my son would be fine.

The drive to Birmingham had been twisty (my dad had taken the countryside route via Bromyard). I felt I needed a night in the hospital just to recover from the journey, I had been texting well-wishers back for most of the trip so felt queasy from doing so. My mum had decided to ride shotgun for the trip for good measure, there was, however, not much conversation in the car, I was focused on keeping positive and focused on the days ahead.

After saying farewells to my parents outside the hospital, Claudia and I strolled through the cavernous foyer and taking the lift full of visitors holding their flowers or magazines and patients in their dressing gowns, we arrived at the seventh floor ward. We were greeted by a gaggle of nurses behind the main ward desk, who pointed us down the corridor to my allocated bed, number 20. It was a bed nearest the door in a room of four beds, with three other patients (inmates), I was the youngest by some 40 years, I estimated. I was immediately sceptical, the only privacy was a curtain on a rail which could be pulled across to screen all sides, the only bathroom facilities was a large wet room come disabled toilet which was shared by the four patients assigned to that room.

Your senses are immediately heightened, hospitals are notoriously noisy, with beeps going on every few minutes warning a nurse (who incidentally maybe nowhere near you), that you have a blockage in your drip line, or that a patient requires attention after, for example, shitting the bed! I quickly spotted people who had advanced symptoms of serious liver illness, the guy opposite me was a totally jaundice colour, yellow all over, even his eye whites were an unhealthy urine colour, yellower than the Sahara desert. Facing me was the man's catheter bag, clearly the man wasn't well, and I was told, later in my visit, that he was dying. Then, there was Clarrance in the bed diagonally opposite, a small man in stature, a lovely and a softly spoken Welshman originally from Neath, probably in his mid-80s by my estimation, a retired teacher and as sharp as a button. Clarrance had internal organ issues after a severe fall and also couldn't walk due to a back injury, he struggled for example to get out of his chair to his bed. Above Clarrance's bed was a sign pointing out the fact he was also suffering from diabetes, and it referred to 'no sugar'. As far as I could tell, the third guy had less to worry about apart from his chronic wind problem, this guy needed the loo every 30 minutes, I estimated he was in early eighties fitter and more nimble than the other two also. The lighting in the wardroom is so bright, with loads of activity, nurses and doctors coming and going, there is always something to arouse your senses. Noise, some activity to look at and of course, various smells emanating from patients or the ward.

Shortly after arriving, I was asked to put on a surgery gown with a nice pair of dark stockings which came up to the knee and had a hole on the underside of the toe, I was told these were to stop deep vein thrombosis. A pretty, female, Indian doctor was my first visitor, checking my personal information and then inserting a cannula into my right arm on the inside side of the elbow. She was very gentle. I was then visited regularly by nurses for observations, temperature, blood pressure, blood sugar and I had, in all, three lots of blood taken.

Psychologically, I was treating this as a challenge, I was treating it as an Olympic sporting event, where, as a competitor having trained daily for four years, I needed to peak at the right time. I felt really good, it didn't seem right to be sliced open the next day but I knew it was necessary and seemingly according to the experts the only way forward for me to survive, continue with life.

That evening was like a farting competition between my roommates, each dropping rumblings from their respective corners, so I joined in occasionally, I seemingly had more control of my wind than these guys. At one point, one of the guys must have shat himself as the stench was atrocious. I did also complain to the male Filipino nurse Bill, that one of my roomies had also left a small deposit on the toilet seat, an unpleasant shit stain. Clearly, Bill didn't think it was his remit to clear it up, it was still there 12 hours later when suddenly, six cleaners arrived at the same time to give the room a refresh.

It is fair to say it was an awful night's sleep but I wasn't here to sleep. Bill fitted a drip into my cannula at 12 p.m. and placed a sign on my drip stand reading Nil by Mouth.

The next morning, I was visited by the anaesthetist who had a brief chat as to what I should expect, I would have a cannula in the back of the hand through which they would knock me out. At that point, they would fit an epidural line to my spine, another cannula into my neck, a nose tube into my stomach and a catheter into my penis (awesome, not!). Before I came back into the world, I would have a drain fitted to the incision to drain any internal bleeding or bile collecting. I would be heavily sedated when I came around, the epidural numbing the full extent of the pain around the wound. This all sounded so unreal, it is difficult to know what to expect when you haven't experienced it before.

Next to see me was a young liver surgeon, kitted out in his blue surgery gown perhaps I pondered on his rounds between operations, he gently felt around my abdomen and said he would see me in theatre. Then, he mentioned, "There is a whiff," he paused to cough, "of a transplant coming in but nothing concrete yet, this is the only thing which could delay your operation!"

I knew from my consultations with the liver team previously that a transplant coming in, due to the critical life or death element effectively gazumps your place in the queue. I knew that might mean a delay for my treatment, I desperately didn't want that to happen, here I was, peaking at the right time and I was ready for this.

Quite soon after the young liver surgeon had left, a guy probably in his late 50s arrived smart-casually dressed, looking more like an artist than a surgeon. This guy was Italian and after pleasantries, felt my stomach and abdomen and then ran gently through using his finger, to indicate on my body, where they would cut me open. It seemed to me, as I listened intently, like a big incision was planned, straight down the middle from the base of my sternum then moving in a line right under my ribs, if you like one massive L shape back to front. I would be needing a lot of tattoo ink to cover this scar and as he was talking, I tried to imagine what a tattoo artist might suggest, perhaps a seal on a sun lounger or a snake with a broken back? I was, apparently, first on the list scheduled to go into theatre at 8:30 a.m. I was ready for it.

At 12 midday, I was still waiting to go into theatre, 8:30 a.m. now a long way in the past. I have never been that patient waiting and this was hard given that I was waiting for a major operation and had been ready to peak at the right time. I was also starving having been nil by mouth for so long.

To take my mind of things, I watched Clarrance, sharp as a button as always. The snack trolley came into our room, pushed by someone who'd I concluded had lost the enthusiasm the job required. As she brought the trolley to a pause in the middle of the room, Clarrance politely asked, in his soft south Wales accent, for a Bakewell slice, Jaffa cake pack and a Kit Kat. At first, I didn't put two and two together, Clarrance took his order creating a neat pile on his bed as the trolley departed. It wasn't until he had scoffed the lot and a ward nurse came in to test his blood sugar I saw the problem. The nurse gently pricked his finger for the blood sugar test and tested the blob of blood immediately, then the nurse started looking concerned almost doubting what she was seeing from the test.

Suddenly, turning to Terrance, she said with a raised voice, "Your blood sugar level is through the roof, how is this possible?" Clarrance was a consummate professional liar and pleaded ignorance as to how this could have come about. *The sly old fox*, I thought, *he didn't own up to his 20 minutes munching through his favourite sugary snacks.* It tickled me, I couldn't stop smiling but I was happy for him, he was enjoying life.

Clarrance spent a lot of his time in his bed but as there was a problem with the electronics, they had put him in the armchair next to the bed and ordered a bed engineer. His bed wouldn't go up or down so it made it uncomfortable for him. After 30 minutes, I witnessed the bed engineer arrive and look at the reference numbers on all four beds, he had a trolley of his own full of tools. There were no nurses about despite literally every buzzer going off in our room, so the bed engineer carried on without consulting whoever had called him out to attend to Clarrance's bed, Clarrance said nothing, neither did I. I imagined the nurses were gathered around the main ward desk, as they had been when we had checked in the day before, chatting about the weekend, the latest episode of *EastEnders* and whatever drama was unfolding.

The engineer wanted to get on with his rounds and seemed to know what he wanted to do and with that, got the chap next to me out of his bed, unplugged it and pulled into the central area of our room. The chap next to me looked bemused as he sat in his armchair, opposite Clarrance, farting away. It took ten minutes to test every angle of the bed (I was amazed how high those babies go!), before the engineer concluded this was a false alarm. It was only as he walked out of the door with his tool bag that I realised, with a wry smile on my face, that the engineer had tested the wrong bed. The sister who came in 20 minutes later asked Clarrance if they had fixed his bed. Clarrance had a long wait in his chair.

At approximately 4 p.m., a 30 something female Spanish nurse came up to my bed and gave my wife and I the news we had suspected might come, unfortunately, they were not going to be able to operate on me today, due to a transplant having come in. I kind of didn't have a problem with that, however she then told us I was being sent home.

I remonstrated, "Surely, I just move down the line of the waiting list to be operated on tomorrow?"

"No," she retorted, "there are people having operations tomorrow."

That was my first realisation that I would be in for a long wait to get back into the NHS system that clearly has its issues with resources and ensuring everyone gets treated on time.

Slightly annoyed, we left without waiting for the discharge papers. I did think perhaps they are still searching for me under bushes in the grounds, treating me as an escapee but I suspect, on second thought, they wouldn't have had the time.

At least my son, Josh, was over the moon to see daddy home. To be honest, I was chuffed to be home too. I loved life. I would have to wait for a new appointment to come through from the NHS, in the interim I left messages for my oncologist to see if there was a faster route privately. I was after all a private patient if I wanted to be, I had put my faith in the NHS and it had let me down, the whiff of a transplant had turned out to be a stink. Whilst that sounds like a moan, I found out that the transplant I had been moved for, was a little boy whose dad was donating part of his liver to save him. I totally saw that, as a liver surgeon, that was more of a priority on the day, it wasn't their fault they didn't have more resources to treat everyone on time.

It didn't take me long to look for the positives. I had gained from the experience a better perspective on what to expect and I had better opportunity to prepare my sons for my next visit. I could get fitter and continue to build my immune through nutrition. I was, as usual, open about the few days experience on Facebook and loved the energy from the positivity people posted, it made me feel alive.

Chapter 22
What Now?

Tom Jackson called me, I had hoped he would call, he was responding to my message the previous week where, after the cancellation of my operation by the NHS, I was questioning him why I couldn't just go private for the operation. One of the first things Tom said was, "Is there any reason why you cannot do an operation before 31st May, as the QE are reporting you are unable to do any date before then due to work commitments?"

"That is absolute rubbish!" I exclaimed with annoyance clearly evident in my voice, "I never said that to them!"

It does make you wonder how someone within the NHS manages to make something like that up, perhaps they needed a valid reason on the system for my operation not having been undertaken within the NHS target period. I was cross, I felt let down but left Tom to go back to the QE and wrestle with them using the private option to try and extract a date sooner than the one scheduled by the NHS. As an oncologist, he should have clout, if needed, drawing on reference to my overall circumstances and vulnerability off chemo and other drugs controlling its spreading.

The next phone call came from a lovely lady at the QE— Sandra, asking if I could come in for my operation on 21st May. This was good, I would go in on a Saturday and have the operation on the Sunday, this time I would be on a private ward, at least for the non-intensive-care bits.

I never really understood why I had gone down the NHS route for the operation when I had the medical insurance scheme through work but clearly, money was talking now, I was jumping waiting lists. I guess my oncologist had had faith in the NHS system and to be fair, if it wasn't for the transplant coming in and resulting in my cancellation perhaps it would have all worked out.

I still had to do the administration part of making the arrangements, speaking to the medical company giving them details of the operation type, surgeon etc. which needed their prior authorisation. I needed from them an authorisation code to give to the QE, in effect authorising payment of the fees and operation costs under the policy. They wouldn't give me one until I had the operation type codes and name of the anaesthetist from the QE. I ended up relaying information over a number of phone calls, eventually, it was sorted and once again, I began looking forward to getting the operation underway.

On 17th May, I met Larry for a couple of Becks Blues over lunchtime. Poor Larry was in a dilemma. Here he was balancing his ex-girlfriend, a monthly hooker, an ex-colleague from the art world and now on the go with a new woman he met on tinder one night after setting a 10-mile search net from his living room. It amazed me that, in this day and age, it was simple to effectively wave a flag with 'I am lonely and horny' on it and work out which eligible females were available within a designated geographical area. This woman was different, it sent his usual priceless, polite but gigolo attitude into sudden disarray. Something about this one he really liked and so far, she hadn't let him go the distance, he was being made to wait it out. I imagined his Cadburys chocolate selection box on standby in his car boot, unopened but ready in case things got kinky really quickly.

Larry was telling me how frustrating it was likely to be for him, trying to behave on the forthcoming evening's date with this mysterious newcomer, needing to show a measured calm and respectful approach instead of going straight in for the bonk and full inspection of a new set of genitals.

It was good, Larry took my mind off things and thinking about the operation. I was more prepared than the last time, ultimately, I was positive, I was still just bloody grateful that an operation was possible, it may easily of not have been. I drifted off into my own thoughts as Larry weighed up his chances of a sexual experience, he was talking about the importance of smell and being comfortable with it during intimacy. My thoughts were looking forward to more privacy this time around with my own room and how I thought I would feel coming around from the anaesthetic. I imagined lots of lights, tubes, noises, pain and

I suspected lucid thoughts, after all, I would be on morphine. I can't say I wasn't interested in this as an experience, it would be totally new to me on so many levels.

I didn't sleep well on the evening of 17th May, my mind was racing plus I had to get up at 4:15 a.m. to get ready for a 5:45 a.m. train ride from Ledbury to London Paddington. I had an important work meeting scheduled for 10:00 a.m. in London. Did I need to be fully up to date with sleep before my operation, I didn't think it mattered. I hoped to catch up on sleep while I recovered, albeit based on the one night's experience courtesy of the NHS, I didn't hold out much hope of that, it was as noisy as a slot machine arcade of a busy Vegas hotel.

I felt really good overall, physically and mentally prepared for what lay ahead. I had been taking natural immune boosters, prescribed to me by my nutritionist Jen. It had to be said despite 16 sessions of chemo, I hadn't had a proper cold since I was diagnosed despite being exposed to plenty of people with horrible colds around me. Nutrition was so important to my journey so far, my recovery and life ahead.

Chapter 23
Nutrition

For most of my life I didn't give nutrition any thought whatsoever. I wasn't a bad eater or a secret Jaffa cake muncher or excessively into any foods or liquids deemed to be totally unhealthy, I just didn't see that changing my diet would make much difference to me. This mind-set changed dramatically on diagnosis, part of me thinking it was like trying to shut the stable gate after the horse had already bolted.

Yes, I drank beer and wine in plentiful supply and ate all sorts of tinned produce at university, like tinned pies and vegetables were more of a Sunday lunch roast dinner accompaniment than a daily ritual but I wasn't totally unhealthy. I tried, for example, throughout my sporting ambitions, to boost performance with say chicken and pasta the night before a hockey game and say an isotonic drink after the game but nothing in any fastidious detail.

Getting diagnosed with cancer was, for me, a turning point and in my view, it wasn't too late. What would I need for energy levels confronting say chemo and a low immune system and anything that would slow the spread. Things would clearly need to change but how would things need to change? I mentioned earlier that my lovely pal Nina, had recommended a nutritionist she had used through serious illness, which she believed was one of the primary changes to have saved her life. Initially, people around you, some meaning well, bombard you with different advice based on their experience of cancer or people they have known with serious illness. I had to weed out the good advice from the bad and nutrition was definitely a positive if I was prepared to embrace it.

Perhaps, with a degree of reluctance, I eventually got my act together whilst balancing my new life of chemotherapy and emailed Jen (the contact Nina had given me). I ended up filling out numerous forms relating to my current eating/drinking habits as well as specifics about my illness. I then had a 20-minute conference call with Jen. It turned out Jen was a specialist in cancer nutrition, having worked with oncologists in the States where nutrition and oncology went hand in hand, Jen also had a fellowship in cancer care. From that very first conversation, I knew this was a massive positive, on the battlefront, this was like adding a special force's sniper to the team in the fight against the enemy cancer. Jen could target specific cancer with different bullets (the extract capsules) and be attacking from all angles based on experience. Jen impressed me with her immediate hunger to win, aiming to target and destroy cells, starving them of nutrients and making it impossible for them to survive whilst continually ensuring yours truly had full resupply of armaments for the war campaign.

I liked Jen's confidence and knowledge. She was thinking immediately how to slow growth, for example cutting refined sugar out of my diet and the insulin in dairy which both apparently promoted cancer cells to grow. So whilst both would need to go, replacement foods would be substituted in its place. For example, coconut sugar would replace refined sugar, goat products, ewe's products or rice/almond milk would replace dairy.

Long lists of target foods were emailed over and immediately with the help of Claudia, my diet transformed immediately and massively. You really must be prepared to embrace the change and look forward to trying new things. So I started eating more organic salmon, chicken with more organic vegetables like broccoli, asparagus, no sauces and for snacks more fruits such as apples, blueberries and almonds. Treats like cakes were still permitted, they just needed to be made with the right ingredients, instead of coco powder, for example, in a chocolate cake, it would be made with raw cacao, coconut syrup and olive oil. To me, it still tasted good.

I had given up alcohol which was hard mentally, caffeine and bread out of choice, so the new diet took a bit of getting used to but so what, if it was contributing to saving my life then it was another weapon against the enemy. There were new curries to try full of turmeric, another spice important to get into my system, black pepper was important to help absorption. I always love curry, eating more of it was a positive. I tried to eat more garlic, certainly only when I didn't have too many meetings the next day. None of us like to stink a meeting room out.

I started eating Manuka Honey, imported from New Zealand, where the bees that make it collect pollen from the manuka/tea tree bushes, their honey being so rich in antioxidants. It is an expensive item but my mum and her sister regularly bought me a pot and I opted for a spoonful a day.

I came across a bar of chocolate I could eat, very small and again pricey but as good as any of the chocolate bars I was missing, if not better and full of none of the refined sugar. Ombar, which came in an assortment of different flavours too. I conceded the money I spent on Ombars I would have spent on wine or beer. There was just the bonus of no hangover.

My diet, I had worked out with Jen, gave me energy and every element was reportedly doing something to fight the cancer, it was a huge positive knowing that diet was a strong weapon in the fight. Psychologically, I liked the idea of confronting the disease as a strategic battle and carefully calculating which weapons I would be using, each aspect would be either play a defensive or attacking role, individually contributing their part, overall making a huge dent in the capability of cancer's own strategic battle hardened, well-drilled plan.

In the early days of my new diet, I had a daily cup of turmeric tea. At first, this was palatable, however, after a few months, I was almost retching each time the cup of yellowish liquid was put in front of me. The drink consisted of a cup of coconut milk, a teaspoon of turmeric, black pepper, a slice of fresh ginger and a spoonful of honey. There came a point where I had to come up with a new way of getting the turmeric into my system and this was the main reason I needed curry, it had to be the way. A curry that allowed a large dose of turmeric but didn't have a high sugar or dairy content. I would fry a small onion, add two cloves of garlic, use chicken or turkey or beef, add the curry powder and turmeric, then 500ml of chicken stock and shavings of coconut block to thicken the sauce. Black pepper was added to help absorption of the turmeric into my blood stream. I concluded, unlike the turmeric tea I would never get bored of curry, I still eat loads of it today. It was the curcumin in turmeric which was so important in the combat of cancer cells, it gives turmeric its yellow colour and in recent media reports, is also proving a key compound in the fight against things like depression.

There were other compounds too which would prove vital in the fight and worthwhile in rolling out in the skirmish against cancer. EGCG was found in green tea, sulforaphane found in broccoli and kale, quercetin found in onions, apples and blackberries, ursolic acid found in blueberries and basil, vitamin D in things like salmon and eggs. Overall, there was nothing in my old diet I missed, I embraced the new foods as a positive and good new addition to my lifestyle.

Chapter 24
Machine Guns at the Door

For the second time around, I journeyed up to Birmingham's QE Hospital with Claudia, my father acting as chauffeur. The Edgbaston suite (the private ward) was located in the old part of the hospital, the entrance tucked off a side road which looped around the hospital, it could also be reached from the new spaceship-like building (the new sections of the QE), by way of a pedestrian link bridge.

On arrival in the ward, I was shown to a large room which had a typical hospital bed, a TV on the wall, an en suite shower room, a small round table with two chairs and an armchair with a footstool. This was a complete contrast to the NHS ward I had been on a few weeks ago, which was more of a communal dormitory. We had arrived at the Edgbaston suite as instructed at 5 p.m., and a lovely male nurse (very camp) had offered us some food, I accepted his offer of some potato wedges. As before, I would be nil by mouth from 12 p.m., and the consultant would drop in to see me that evening to run through procedures for the following day. The consultant surgeon, Sami, was lovely, I couldn't think of a better person to perform such a major operation on me, such a positive character.

Sami did, indeed, see me that evening and ran through what would happen. To a certain extent, he already knew what to expect when he got into the abdominal cavity from his analysis of the CT and MRI scan results, however, if it was a different scenario once inside, they would do what was necessary in terms of removal of scar tissue, lesions and tumours. They would ultrasound the liver once I had been opened up. After a calm and polite conversation, Sami departed and I felt relaxed and ready for the next day. Claudia also left to go to accommodation within the hospital complex nearby, I was alone and left pretty much to my own devices with the exception of visits from a doctor to fit a cannula and nurses monitoring me.

Shortly after waking the next morning, Claudia arrived from her stay in visitor accommodation located over the road and the anaesthetist also arrived to give me a run-down of what to anticipate. John Scott was in his operating blues, we ended up talking about hockey, he like me, was a keen hockey player, the conversation put me at ease.

I was in my gown and my green surgery stockings (I imagined necessary to prevent blood clots and thrombosis) not long having said my goodbyes to the anaesthetist, when the porters arrived in no time at all, to wheel me the seemingly endless journey down corridor after corridor to the theatre preparation area. Claudia walked alongside the bed as it was negotiated along the route, a porter at each end. The guy at the front of my bed was older and didn't seem to be doing very much other than being a real character chaperoning my bed and the route ahead, a proper brummie and offering vocal banter to anyone he passed going in the opposite direction. On one section of the epic journey down the hospital corridors and at the start of a seemingly vast corridor with no apparent end to it, a huge figure appeared at the other end. This mountain of a man was sauntering towards us. The guy must have been 7ft tall and not without muscles either.

"Here he is!" shouted my brummie porter, "My bodyguard," he exclaimed. I was thinking, I do hope you know him, I don't want any more delays this close to surgery.

In the room outside of the main theatre, a theatre nurse ran through my medical history again along with my vital information, just to check they had the right patient. It occurred to me they must do this due to the wrong people getting the wrong operation in the past. How bad would that be to go in for say a knee operation and come out having had a lung removed. I had to give contact information should something not go according to plan and with that, I said my goodbyes to Claudia who, until that time, had held my hand, I was then wheeled away into a small room where John the anaesthetist was waiting. We again chatted about hockey, he then cleared the cannula with a flush as we were speaking, a saline solution was injected and then I guess the knock out juice as I can only remember chatting about hockey and then coming around post operation. That simple.

I was now in recovery, a room with a nurse by my side, I wasn't in pain and I established I was heavily sedated and a bit drowsy. There was none of the panic, 'where am I?' and 'what are these tubes?' kind of thinking, I was comfortable and aware of where I was and what was happening. I had come through major liver surgery and out the other side, it was now about the critical phase of things healing and working normally and avoiding infections, with close monitoring by professionals.

After a short period of maintaining my vital signs in the recovery bay, I was then moved to ICU (Intensive Care Unit), the bed post from the ceiling read A26, I noted how high-tech this part of the hospital was and a lot of the nurses were serving military personnel, the nurse looking after me, Mack, being a Royal Navy nurse. Mack was doing a fantastic job giving me Oramorph (a painkiller containing Morphine Sulfate) and other intravenous drugs to dull any pain. Claudia was, again, suddenly by my side for reassurance and overall, I was feeling relaxed, the epidural obviously doing its job numbing the area where the incision had been. I had two drains, effectively plastic pipes expelling gunk and fluid from my abdominal cavity just above my pelvis one on my left and one on my right side. I had a central line cannula in my neck, a blood pressure/gas monitor in my artery in my right wrist, a cannula in my right arm opposite my elbow and of course, a good old catheter which took away the sensation to urinate, my bladder making those decisions on its own. It took me a while to work out that I was just continually urinating without any conscious effort on my part or instructions from my brain or sensation of doing so.

I can't remember the exact time but my wonderfully talented liver surgeon popped by confirming everything had gone well and that the team operating on me and primarily, the man stood before me had removed 25% of my liver. I remember staring for a moment at him imagining the mass of damaged organ being passed around as they detached it from my innards and put the bits I was keeping back into place.

Within 24 hours of the operation, Mack had me sat in an armchair for about 30 minutes, it did take a lot of effort given my abdominal muscles had been sliced in two and I got exhausted easily, the anaesthetic and painkillers still coursing through my veins. I also managed a surreal moment of doing a crossword puzzle with Claudia whilst in ICU, I was determined to sit up and do it.

It was about 10:30 p.m. Monday evening 30 plus hours after my admission to intensive care, that two female Filipino nurses from ICU wheeled me to my new residence, the Edgbaston ward which I had checked into some 48 hours plus ago. We chatted en route, we discussed the Philippines (I had good memories of both Manila, the rice terraces to the north and a special island called Boracay located to the south only accessible by boat). One of the nurses was so glad I had been to Boracay, it wasn't that big an island or on the main tourist route, a real hidden gem.

The room I had been allocated on my return to Edgbaston suite, was much smaller, a fraction of the size of the old one, however, at least it had its own en suite. I hadn't been for a number two since before the operation so I was looking forward to toilet privacy, if I could make it out of bed that was and start using my bowels and bladder normally again. I had enquired in ICU about having a number two if the need arose and was told that it would either be a case of doing it in the bed or in a commode chair. *Fuck that,* I thought, an en suite was preferred, so I was happy more for the en suite than any other aspect of the room, no matter how hard the effort to get to the loo.

The room, however, was so hot. The temperature outside the hospital was very warm, it seemed that Britain was experiencing a mini-heat wave. The room had no air conditioning given it was in the old section of the hospital and for a patient with constipation, numerous tubes sticking out of me and the inability to move much, this was hard to endure. Another issue was Edmund, a neighbouring patient I became aware of on my first night. I couldn't see Edmund, but, Christ, through the walls, I could hear him! Any patient in a hospital bed has a call button, once you press it, you can hear the regular buzzer going off both next to your bed and on the desk of the nurse station along the corridor. The only way the nurse can turn it off is to come and see the patient and manually turn it off next to your bed. It appeared Edmund was determined not to use his buzzer. This noisy loud and uncouth, possibly Australian/Jordy, accented individual, would simply shout, 'help, help, help, help,' until he got attention. Sometimes, it would be for ages with no response—'my head hurts, nurse, nurse, my head hurts'. This went on sometimes literally all night. I heard one patient lose it with Edmund and some of the nurses. It was like having a spoilt pensioner, very demanding and needy too close for comfort. I did complain and did, at one point, think of going into Edmund's room and offering to deport him by my own methods during the dead of night to Australia.

The hardest day post-operation was Wednesday 24th, when, after my consultant had agreed to it in the morning, three nurses (one a student), opted to start the process to remove my various tubes, in one go. I was keen for this to be done, it would, after all, give me more independence, not having to cart bags of fluid around with my piss, gunk and blood gunge. Clearly, I was an ideal guinea pig for training student nurses, having five tubes or lines which needed removal.

The trio discussed the best course and opted for the least painful tube removal first in their combined view. The catheter. Easy to say, it's not painful if you are a woman but as a man, it was the one I was least looking forward to. I just remember the one nurse telling the other, 'you just pull and it gradually comes out'. 'Wait a minute, ladies' I was saying in my mind, 'this is my cock we are talking about!' Perhaps she is right but by pulling it I soon discovered it felt like someone was trying to pull your cock off, literally. To avoid the pain and the prospect of having to have my cock sewn back on, I had to grab the base of my cock simultaneously to the nurse pulling the tube, this at least felt like I had stopped it being pulled off, this didn't, however, prevent the sensation that the insides were being pulled out. This was more uncomfortable than painful in sensation and apparently, if I couldn't urinate within the next six hours, they would have to insert it back into me, to avoid me unnecessarily storing urine. *Jesus!* I thought, *no one is going near it again, I will be urinating for sure!*

The next on their list was the drain on my right side, they snipped open the stitches that held it in place and the senior nurse of the trio, started pulling. I was expecting pain but the epidural on that side of my body clearly helped. Out it came with small bother, I was, however, surprised how much pipe there had been inside me. The epidural was next to be removed and I hardly felt that coming out, followed by the neckline. It, again, surprised me how long that needle was and the fact it was in a major vein towards my heart.

The only thing left now was the drain on my left side, again they undid the small stich holding it in place and under instruction the student nurse started pulling it slowly. Too slowly in my view, they told me to take deep breaths which I did but this was a long pipe right up into my abdominal cavity and clearly settled in its position. I imagined it happy in its position resting against my internals cemented in place by congealed gunk and puss. I wasn't wrong! It honestly felt like my organs, especially my liver where it felt like the end of the tube was attached to, were being pulled downwards towards my pelvis. This made me feel like I was bruising internally a weird unnatural pain that made me feel queasy. The tube eventually emerged with a smack of the lips sounds, gunk and blood flying all over the place. This was definitely worse than having the catheter removed and the worst pain in the process to date.

I spent the next six hours eagerly trying to urinate as normal, I reverted to running taps, trying to get the sound of running water to stimulate the process, even whistling loudly to hit that perfect note which stimulates urination. Incidentally, at this point, I remained constipated and all I could hear from next door was Edmund shouting ' help, help, help', like a helpless seal pup abandoned on the beach during killer whale lunch time free for all.

With all my tubes removed, I was now happy to receive visitors and this started with some pals from work, Lisa one of the girls in my team and Chet, a fellow director. I had to apologise to visitors in respect of the heat in the room, it was like something out of a scene from the English patient, some overseas hospital bed in extremely hot, humid climate.

On the Thursday, Claudia had come in as usual at 11ish and known to her but unknown to me, a great pal, Ewey, was scheduled to pop in at 2 p.m. to surprise me. Surprise visitors are great, Claudia went off for a bit while Ewey and I had a proper catch up. I was godfather to one of Ewey's sons and vice versa. I was, however, tired and still constipated and apparently, nodded off during his visit. It was difficult getting regular sleep, with nurses checking vital signs through the night, bringing medication and then taking blood samples every morning at 6:00 a.m. Edmund didn't assist matters with his regular 'my head my head, nurse, nurse'.

I apologised to Ewey for nodding off and after saying farewell, he left at 3:45 p.m. So far, the day was progressing normally and at 5 p.m., another mate, Deano, arrived for a catch up. Again, Deano is Godfather to one of my sons as I am to his daughter. Following another catch up, where I stayed awake this time, Deano left after 45 minutes. Everything was normal so far, I was enjoying seeing people.

At 6:30 p.m., Emily, a friend and colleague from work, arrived, slightly later than schedule (Emily was covering all bases with me being off work) and at the same time, TJ made me aware he was on the hospital campus ready to see me once Emily had left. Emily and I ran through various work projects, we had just found out we had been successful in our pitch to retain a portfolio beating all competitors. I, again, apologised to Emily for the heat, Edmund and now a new annoyance, a low flying police helicopter hovering outside my window. I said my goodbyes to Emily at about 7:10 p.m. and TJ then arrived pretty much at that point. I settled in for proper catch up with TJ, who had driven up from his barracks near Marlborough where TJ had just taken on his new job as a Lt Colonel.

It was at that point something weird happened.

Claudia phoned me to say Emily (who had just left my bedside), had been in contact by phone and was stuck in the hospital, the QE being in lock down. Firstly, to me at that moment, it seemed a very strange thing for Emily to have phoned Claudia but I said I would phone her to see if she wanted to come back to the room.

Emily picked up right away and told me that the hospital was literally crawling with armed police, they were searching for a man with a rucksack who had failed to stop when challenged by security. Somewhere within this vast hospital, the suspect was now at large playing cat and mouse with the police. In the meantime, Emily had, indeed, been passed from armed guard to armed guard and was currently hiding in a kitchen with ten nurses, they were being told to stay there. According to Emily, it was a stuffy, cramped and hot environment with limited communication as to what was happening. There was no chance of Emily making it back to the room.

I finished the call and relayed the information to TJ. He smiled, after all this was his domain, bombs, terrorism and guns. I didn't think he was carrying a weapon (usually a 9mm sig) but within seconds, he had stuck his head out of the door to check what was happening. Beckoning the attention of a ward sister, TJ informed her he was an army officer if they needed any assistance, she, however, politely informed him to stay in the room until further notice, it appeared we, too, were in lockdown until more was known.

As we listened to the low flying police helicopter circling outside, its rotors cutting the air with a deafening *thrump thrump* as it turned direction, its twin engines screaming, we sat grinning almost like old times, the risk factor, excitement there once again. That hint of risk, like thinking about linking arms over the roof of a car as in the old days.

"This could be a bloke with a bomb or weapon, hospitals are down as targets this weekend, it reported it on the news," I said informatively, "however, I am in no fit state to be running out of his way, in this condition." TJ seemed comfortable but wasn't suggesting we barricade the room door just yet.

After a while of just listening, there was a degree of commotion just outside my door, people running, I then heard Marian, one of the nurses who had been looking after me, say, "The man they are looking for is sat just outside the ward here." Just to the side of my door was the back entrance to the Edgbaston Ward, a security code accessed door which led to a long sky bridge downward style ramp leading to the new hospital. Just where the doors to the ward were, were a set of comfy chairs and a table. It was here that Marian thought the suspect was seated. It kind of made sense given that if you are on the run, moving away from the main hospital that is a likely route to the old hospital network and potentially an exit route. However, given the doors to the ward were security coded, the suspect would not have been able to go any further.

There was more running past my window, this time the black and white of police hats, men in a three quarter crouched position moving stealthily, then they opened the back door to the ward simultaneously as more police officers emerged from another door to surround their target and suspect. We listened to the armed police '…get your hands out in front and lay face down', or something to that effect.

TJ, again, offered his services peeking both ways down the corridor, this time telling them about his role in bomb disposal and counter terrorism, they took more interest this time but the police seemed to have ten armed men around the suspect and had things under control. It made me think if the suspect had detonated a bomb, we would have been toast, covered in glass fragments, big chunks of wall and ceiling not to mention the metal assortments collected and forming part of the bomb itself, to cause more harm. It was only four days after the Manchester attack so it was not only a distinct possibility but a reality that this could happen somewhere like the QE.

Ironically, both TJ on entering the ward and Emily on exiting the ward, had walked past the suspect. Instead of nurses, police now populated the area outside my room. Was this yet another case of living life on the edge, getting close to game over for me and one of my buddies, it certainly felt like it at the time!

Chapter 25
Banter

A lot of communications with my close mates were on either WhatsApp, messenger or text message. It had been an important part of taking my mind off things even if some of the banter from my male friends was about some of my side effects or conditions of my illness, I loved it. The below is excerpts from a WhatsApp group called St Ives Crew.

Immediately, after my liver surgery was a period of constipation and despite enduring laxatives morning and night, nothing in the hospital was working. Primarily, I understood from the medical staff, when you have a liver operation, it is necessary to move the bowel and, rightly so, the bowel doesn't like being handled. It can shut down. Here is an example of my pals and their response to this news, 25th May—the operation was on 21st May.

Me: despite my room being 100 degrees and feeling like I have been poisoned and raped by a walrus at the same time, positive I don't have a strong pressure rate but I am pissing. I am looking forward to more visitors today and laying the longest turd which I have saved since Saturday. Thing is, my abdominal muscle control all of that, so could take a while.

TJ: I almost passed out the first crap I had after my appendix came out!!!!

Digger: That's going to be one seriously big shit!

Me: I'll send you a photo!

Digger: It's OK, mate. I'll believe you.

Me: No, seriously, it's a pleasure honestly.

Next day, when TJ was visiting me in the hospital:

Digger: I'm dying to know. Have you had that shit yet and did you make TJ witness it?

TJ responds with a picture of an empty loo—'no sign of one there, mate'.

Digger: For a split second, I thought you had actually sent a picture of your mammoth shit.

Me: Too busy to crap, for some reason, the hospital is in lock down.

TJ: TV cameras outside the hospital!

Digger: Must be waiting for Stanley's had a shit announcement.

A few days later…

Me: Where could this shit be?? Apparently, I get laxatives tomorrow. Be thankful with a 30 degree heat it isn't your day to visit me. This room will be a health hazard zone.

Digger: I'm sure it will surface soon! That incident of QE lockdown all over the press.

Me: We should sell our story, TJ, or go on the front page of the Hereford Times 'Friends caught up in lock down constipation nightmare'.

Digger: I think that is a shit idea.

TJ: How is that shit coming along???

Me: I have taken loads of laxatives and still no sign. I have eaten loads of food. I may burst first.

Digger: Hospital laxatives don't fuck around, quicker than the over counter stuff. When that shit starts coming, nothing is going to stop it, so brace yourself, mate.

Me: I hope not, I have visitors all afternoon!! Apparently because they handled my bowel, it goes into lockdown mode, suppository next I am told.

TJ: It'll be like that scene from *'Dumber and Dumber'*.

Me: I don't have the muscle capacity to push, so I hope it will just go for it on its own accord.

Digger: I wouldn't fancy being the nurse that gives you the suppository, could unleash a hell of a mess. P.S only other idea I have, is neck six pints of Old Rosie, in like nectar, out like butter. I haven't drunk that stuff again since I shit myself.

Me: Still no shit. I am going to try some cherries, given the gestation period, should I name this turd?

Digger: Geronimo!

27th May

Digger: Any update on that turd??

Me: Despite significant laxatives, it still won't come! I am risking a car journey home with parents. Hopefully, I won't redecorate the inside of the car.

Digger: Two positives there 1) I always said you were full of shit, and now I am vindicated. 2) You are not travelling back in your car, so no problem.

28th May

I send a picture of a pack of suppositories.

Me: Still no shit! Are they having a laugh!! Bullet shaped suppositories!

Digger: Enjoy!

Me: It's up there. That's a new experience, feels like I have a pen up my arse! Waiting now, pants off, I'm ready.

Digger: Not sure they work that quickly!

Me: Nothing yet!

TJ: Broadsword calling Danny Boy, has the eagle landed yet???

Digger: pssst, TJ, have you got any bangers? I am thinking of planting one outside his lounge and scaring him shitless!!

Me: I inserted suppository and it did prompt me to pass a shit that looked like and was the size of a pear!

TJ: Did you cry??

30th May

Me: Well, my bowels finally opened naturally. Not a snaking 2ft length of gleaming brown, more like a couple of plates of thick dark Rogan Josh stuck to the side. Took a few flushes to shift that bad boy!

Digger: Phew, I can feel the relief from Ipswich.

Me: I imagine you will smell it soon too!

31st May

Digger: Has that turd made any more progress??

Me: Another turd tonight, becoming a regular occurrence!

On the 1st June, I send a picture of my scar to the WhatsApp group St Ives Crew—TJ, Digger and me. The wound is leaking heavily at the lowest point of the scar, despite the rest of it having healed well.

TJ: How are you doing, Stanley?

Me: Still leaking, I'm in and out of surgery clinic daily, have had to book appointments for Saturday and Sunday too, out of hours.

Digger: Are they going to postpone taking the staples out?

TJ: Ooooh…that'll be fun, I'm sure, let's hope you don't split in half!!!!!!!

6th June—time for the staples to come out.

Digger: Good luck with the stitches today, mate!

Me: Just had them out. 50 which are exactly the same as office staples in design. No easy way other than nurse pulls them out with a waggle motion and staple remover. Painful process. Done now.

Digger: Ouch, at least it's done now!

Me: Good test of someone's pain barrier. All you can do is control breathing as the tool presses down on the wound, the staple metal being pulled through an already sensitive site.

Digger: I cannot imagine how much that hurt, especially knowing you had more to come out. It's over now, another step forward…

TJ: My work is so dull today, I'm considering heading to the stationary cupboard and having a go with the staplers myself…

Digger: I once zipped the end of my dick through my jean zipper. I imagine the pain is similar. I only wear button fly trousers now!

Me: Yes, painful!

Digger: I had to have 11 stitches in my cock with the zipper incident, very embarrassing turning up at A and E with blood all around my crotch. Got seen quickly though, having stitches out was something else! Nurse was trying hard not to laugh.

Me: Sounds to me like Digger had the wrong hole, not a zipper incident! Or maybe you do have a big cock!

Digger: Gwen is always telling me I am a big cock!!!

Me: I have to say, I thought you had a big cock when you did your naked knee boarding. Certainly scarred the family on the beach!

Digger: Yes, a great example of the immaturity of my friends having to take the piss by towing me five times around the estuary rather than once that was clearly agreed. I am a vindictive cunt and will get you back for that!

Me: I was just an observer!

Digger: A true mate would have stopped it after the second naked tour of the estuary.

Me: In my defence, I was laughing too much, any movement of that sort, I could have fallen overboard.

Digger: I was overboard, it was spring not summer and it was fucking freezing, I couldn't jump off because you were going too fast and I would have castrated myself. Really embarrassing with the neighbours too!

Chapter 26
Dream and You Shall Fulfil

Everything we do, as humans, stems from thought and you ultimately have control of those thoughts. Thoughts themselves link into actions, the directions we take in life and form how we achieve goals. Sometimes, it takes effort to turn thoughts into actions and a lot of dedication but it is absolutely amazing what can be achieved. Yes, I can do this!

I have always looked forward and I worked out early on the positive impact on emotion, taking a thought or good idea and turning it into an action. Sometimes, not complex things, it could be today I will arrange a spontaneous BBQ and invite some pals over. The actually doing it and ending that day having really enjoyed it and feeling positive.

I was a bit of a daydreamer, I could think something, fine tune it in my mind, then imagine it in detail and then implement it pretty much as it had occurred. The more complex thoughts were things like, I want to achieve this in my career by say 25, be driving this type of car and living in this type of house. Getting married, having kids etc. The ideas had to be realistic but were always positive as to where I wanted to take things. It was like road map in my brain and I still use it today. The more I used this process, the more I had good times. The thirst for high jinx times when I was younger, taking risk and living on the edge to more logical things more risk averse aims later in life and ones where I knew they would result in happiness.

Sometimes, these thoughts took time to format, to work out, sometimes days, weeks, months but whether work, personal life, family, friends or financially motivated once set out they were worked towards. It's a bit like looking at the sky in the morning and seeing clouds that slowly clear away to reveal a beautiful blue sky and there is your idea, the clarity and positivity you can aim for.

With this process comes experience in doing it, working positive thoughts into positive actions or results. Thinking I have only just met you but I like you and you are the type of person I want in my life, you're a positive and that is what I intend to surround myself with. Not only like-minded people who want a good time like me but just people and things that make you happy.

So taking this formula, if you do get a negative experience like the massive impact of life changing news, your thought process kicks in. Maybe cloudy at first but then a clear blue-sky road map to looking for the positivity and what actions can be achieved to go ultimately where you want to go. I am not saying this is without difficulty clearly, some life events are almost impossible but there are those chinks of blue to push towards, small steps at first until you are running free towards happier times.

The best advice I could give someone, is look forward not back, look for the positives and try and avoid the negatives, focus on being happy and safe. The mind is so powerful, it needs you to channel its focus to thrive on positive people and experiences. If we can then feel the resulting energy, really catch the wave of positivity that rises from within, we can start to transform to feel alive and stand a better chance of conquering the world and any problems we need to overcome.

Sometimes, we just need to flick that switch in our minds from a negative position to a positive one, just as with a car when we change up a gear we feel more power. You are in the driving seat, simply get on with it. Life is so exciting if we want it to be, we have to accept life is not forever but it is the most precious thing we have as humans, live every second as though it was your last, surrounding yourself with positive people and experiences. I strongly believe this will lead to much better enjoyment of life, new experiences, particularly stimulate the mind and stimulate positive emotion, find your inner energy.

If you are able to turn something that, once upon a time, your mind would have interpreted as a negative experience into a positive one, that is a great skill to develop. As with my illness and the sessions of chemo, biopsies, operation procedures etc. I flicked the switch to positive, these were new experiences, new challenges, positive new experiences to learn from and conquer,

I could have looked at it negatively but what would be the point, these were positives as best as I could make them be.

Chapter 27
Focus and Distraction

Let's face it, we all have things going on in our lives from time to time that we need a break from, maybe it's just something heavy at work or something very emotional in your personal life but having something outside of whatever it is can be a very welcome distraction. If not a distraction, a focus to take your attentions away from having to deal with the problem issues in your mind constantly.

Whilst I had a good positive attitude to the cancer and treatment in my mind, it was still a real help to have the focus of work and things like the mancave as day-to-day things to think about. A focus can be something day to day like this but it can also be a long-term aim to fix on and look towards achieving. People having to deal with a big something in their lives may, for example, focus on looking forward to spending time with their family, wife and kids when they get through it, or spending time with someone who has been there for them through their ordeal, that unique someone, a special person. It may simply be a holiday to look forward to or getting back into hobbies or sports previously enjoyed. Whatever it is, it is so important to have those focuses and positives to either do daily or to look forward to, they will help you get through whatever it is you are dealing with.

After getting diagnosed with cancer and having undergone a few months of treatment, I got all of my various policies out including mortgage policy documents, I wanted to see if anything covered me for my illness in terms of a payout. I hadn't been diagnosed as terminally ill, it was more the term critically ill that seemed to apply. One policy taken out in the 90s to cover our then mortgage endowments, paid out in the event of a diagnosis of a critical illness like cancer. It was a simple, monthly payment type thing and surprisingly, one we had decided to cancel when we moved house, having at that time taken out new policies to cover a repayment mortgage. For some reason, my wife had written the letter cancelling the direct debit but the letter never got sent. I remember looking at the letter thinking, is this a copy, the policy can't be still running can it? To my amazement, it was!

Excited with this new distraction, I wrote to the insurance company and in the first instance, updated our address details. Once I was sure they acknowledged my existence as a policyholder at our current address, I notified them of the illness and how it seemed to perfectly correlate to the criteria for a payout detailed in their policy document. I wasn't sure but these days, I doubt you would get wording so blatantly clear on diagnosis of simply cancer. I was expecting a hundred and one questions and proof of this and that but on receipt of a letter from my oncologist confirming I did, indeed, have cancer of the bowel spread to the liver, with no hesitation they paid out a generous sum.

My bank account suddenly felt the best it had been and it felt like a massive positive as I waded through the sessions of chemo. I had also just got a full refund on my bankcard for a holiday I had booked to Northern Cyprus prior to the diagnosis. Happy days!

I told a few close pals about my new riches, and as any bloke would, pondered buying something you might not normally buy, unless you were, for example, retiring or seriously ill. Discussing things through with Digger, he rationalised with me that provided I didn't spend all of the money, it might be a good idea to look at that classic car I had always wanted. Since a child in the late 70s early 80s watching Stephanie Powers in Heart to Heart and then as a teenager watching Glynis Barber in Dempsey and Makepeace in the late 80s, early 90s (both women I admired and fancied), I was fixated by a car that was iconic in both TV series and spanned both sides of the Atlantic ocean. The Mercedes SL, the shape of the classic SL spanning from the early 70s to the last facelift version in 89. I wanted one and now, I had cash to secure one. This was a well-built iconic legend and would be a good investment if I looked after it.

Digger was keen to be part of the process and we both did a bit of digging on line. One example stood out, it had a full service history and was being sold by a classic car dealer in Rugby. It was in a smokey, platinum silver colour and was the facelift version. Prices varied immensely from 5k for a 1970s in need of work project to low mileage prestige face-lift examples fetching closer to 100k. This was a great distraction and Digger and I made the journey in his new Range Rover cross-country to Rugby.

The moment I saw her, I fell in love, her sexy lines, something erotically timeless like a beautiful woman naked in a sultry curvaceous pose. After a test drive for a few miles, we negotiated a price to include delivery to my home address, the deal was done. The SL was the 420, a V8 and in terms of the production run, a lot rarer than the V6 300 SL version. I was happy I had a new distraction and fulfilled a life-long ambition to own one.

One particularly annoying side effect of the drugs and regular chemo/Cetuximab sessions was damage to my feet. The skin got really thin and they would split easily on places like the heel or big toe, sometimes vertical cuts similar to deep paper cuts in appearance and as painful. I had one on my heel at one time which was about four cm long, extremely irritating and of course, the cuts prevented me being so mobile. It hurt to walk too far.

I was explaining this to Digger one day and that I missed walking the dog and he came up with an idea that using quad bikes we could do a perimeter patrol of his estate, he had been plagued by trespassers and given his woodlands and farmland of some 400 acres it would take some time to navigate the boundaries. I imagined this was not a must do task for Digger, more a kind gesture to get me out and it succeeded in becoming something to look forward to, it was scheduled for the following Saturday. On the Tuesday, I received a call from Digger. A local man had stormed out of his home and in a depressed state had not returned, people were worried about him and police and mountain rescue teams were already scrambled to look for him including a helicopter with thermal imaging. This would be another reason to search Digger's land thoroughly, the man could be injured somewhere and as he only lived a short distance away, it was a distinct possibility.

My training suddenly kicked in, we had done land searches, river searches regularly at the search and rescue centre and I wanted to put that training to good use. Clearly, harder if you cannot walk but even on a quad bike we could cover a large area and search obvious places he may be. The guy was a runner, we had a description of his clothing and knew he was potentially suicidal. My worry approaching that evening was that it was literally minus 8 degrees outside. Too cold to be out in a hilly mountainous area without a good insight into survival techniques. The only plus point was that the guy did have medical training so if injured could deal with certain conditions applying his knowledge.

I wanted to get going on this but it was tricky, we were both working and the daylight was restrictive, really only effective between 8:30 a.m. to 4 p.m. If we were going to operate outside of these times, we would need really powerful torches and even then, the search would not be as thorough, we could miss vital information. Also, I needed to be careful, on chemo your immune can be weaker and if you get injured it can take longer to get over a simple cut, in essence, your body takes longer to heal and is more prone to infection. Bombing around woodland at night time, on a quad, in the state I was in, I would be looking for trouble. We opted to keep our scheduled weekend search time, even though this would be several days after the day the guy disappeared.

A few days went by and the media were reporting that nothing had yet been discovered by the local search teams or helicopter, despite extensive searches, there were even rumours that the chap had fled to the South West where he had connections. I personally wasn't convinced that Digger's land had been thoroughly searched, the guy was used to running around this area and probably had regular trails he used to get away from life and up into the woods, this was an extensive area and given its close proximity to the last known sighting, ideally needed hundreds of searchers/volunteers to scour the landscape.

As the weekend and Saturday approached, I was eager to put my skills to the test, we had discussed where we would start and how we would search using the quads, in reality, we knew that given the number of days that had elapsed, we might be looking for a dead body. All my efforts and thoughts that week were gearing up for Saturday trying to help find the missing person, try and find some answers for those desperately concerned family and friends of the individual.

The day before we were scheduled to go, two hunters found the body which was on Digger's land. It seemed the guy had run a short distance, turned off the main road that linked the villages and found a small copse close to the road. There he had committed suicide, hanging himself from a tree. Bodies deteriorate quickly and this was some four days after the missing person call went out. Digger was glad we hadn't been the ones to stumble across the body, I felt sorry for the fact the relatives and friends would be facing the fact the guy had died in this way but I was otherwise disappointed we hadn't been out earlier searching, this was an area we would have gone to first on our planned search, not that it would have altered the outcome.

It made me think, that some people have a huge amount on their shoulders and cannot cope with it, their need is to just get out of life to ease the burden. I was thinking that people diagnosed with cancer may find themselves in this low spiral not wanting to endure months or years of treatment they consider pointless or painful or degrading. For some, taking your own life is the answer and solution. Whatever the man in the woods had going on, he was at his lowest ebb, he had reached the point where it had to end quickly.

I had always thought positively, searched for the positive points in anything even in the face of seemingly totally negative news, I could never see myself in that scenario. I knew people in my life who had committed suicide, a kid I had grown up with in Leominster took his own life very early on in his late teens, I never knew why and then a lovely guy married to one of my wife's mates, seemingly happy from the external appearances perspective, a father of three kids recently took his life in his early 40s. In his case, he struggled with depression and whatever the trigger, he needed to stop the mental torture. Mental illness is a disease and we all need to be aware of it. I have always tried to be there for people I know who suffer from mental issues, bipolar or manic depression, a few of my mates are in this category. I tried often to instil my throngs of positive vibes, listening, giving an alternative positive perspective on their negative take on a life situation, sometimes, it fell on deaf ears, sometimes, we'd end up having a laugh.

Looking forward to something can be an amazingly powerful thing, something that, in your mind, is so strong a vision or thought, that even if you had the worst done to you, it would still inspire you to look forward, reach for the stars and achieve what you want to achieve. Sometimes, it may seem impossible, unrealistic but if you find those wondrous things to look forward to or maybe it's a special person, it can be a key to your survival and you are lucky to have them.

During my illness, I wanted to do something for a cancer charity, I had this burning ambition inside me to organise something, there were people suffering in far worse positions than me with cancer and I kept thinking how hard having cancer must be for a child. Imagine all those brilliant things you do in your childhood, look forward to in your own magical world, suddenly smashed by something you truly don't fully understand but has landed on you. Like everyone who gets it, you have to get on with the process but things like the side effects must be so much harder at a young age and these drugs are strong things. Losing hair for someone young due to cancer and its treatment, struck me as such a hard thing for a child to contemplate. In my search for a worthwhile charity, I came across, a local charity set up in memory of a little girl who died of cancer. I gave the charity a ring and after speaking to some lovely people, settled on a charity idea, a vehicle clue hunt spanning a number of counties. I would try and raise as much money as possible and get people I knew involved either while I was still being treated or if I made a recovery. It was a good thing to distract my attentions from my journey and focus my mind on something different.

Chapter 28
The Malverns

Having gone from a sigmoid cancer, with multiple bilobar liver metastases inoperable at the time, to having major liver surgery, 30 plus hours in intensive care and six days in hospital, I was working full time from home within two and a half weeks. It was difficult to imagine what had gone on in my body during surgery.

I had a large reverse L shaped scar after my liver operation, held together with 50 staples, which needed to be removed within two weeks of the operation. They were getting painful and sore, especially around where the wound had leaked on the entry points for each staple. It is your GP nurse who typically removes the staples, and surprisingly, a surgical staple looks a lot like an office staple (perhaps a bit bigger and thicker), these are removed with a device that looks a lot like an office staple remover too! That might sound painful as there is no anaesthetic for removal and I won't lie, it is an unpleasant experience. As I lay on a couch on the rolled out paper sheet in my GP nurse's room, hidden behind a feeble curtain, I had my shirt undone and didn't know what to expect. The nurse said, "Are you ready?"

"Yes, I am, let's do it," I responded nervously.

I wasn't ready…I watched the staple remover tool approach my highest staple just below my sternum, the nurse just grabbed the staple with the tool and pulled in a twisting motion. I was watching this and instantly feeling pain. My mind needed to adapt, I asked the nurse for a moment, and closed my eyes, a move which was clearly better than witnessing the process. I could then concentrate on breathing, breathing through the pain. Pain was noticeably different with long breaths in, focusing on that deep breath as each staple came out. The nurse got in a rhythm and yes, some were more painful than others, especially those sore from where my wound had leaked but within a few minutes, 50 staples were out, it was done.

Once the staples were out, I needed to revisit the nurse for daily dressings as the wound was still leaking a bit at its lowest point and also to treat slight over granulation, this was a chore, the wound was taking its time to stop leaking, the nurse primary concern being infection. Granulation around a wound is where as part of the healing process new connective tissue forms, it's in essence proud flesh hanging like globules on the edge of the wound. I was, however, strong and positive and now very eager to get on with treating the bowel, the primary cancer that had caused all of this. It had been put on the back burner by everyone as they concentrated on the more serious issue of the liver.

I thought back to the original bowel sigmoidoscopy and the surgeon turning to me and saying in a big breath, heart-stopping moment, "It's a good job you are here!" as the smooth curve of my watery colon turned into the Malvern Hills, a bumpy raised section of my inner bowel/colon wall in HD with signs of blood at its base. Where it had all started, where my life had to adapt quickly to a new course, the start of a journey.

I often drove back from work after that day, that initial diagnosis, looking at the Malvern Hills, they were silhouetted like lumps of crafted iron rising high, almost placed unnaturally against the settling evening sky. The hills were similar in shape to the bowel tumour, just suddenly looming there above the beautifully sculpted flat landscape below. It represented something to be respected, in a similar way to how I had always had respect for the river or sea, weather or fire. I would stare, as the hills appeared, at first, far off in the distance as I travelled south on the M5. I was in awe of their magnificent presence turning towards Hereford off the Worcester South junction. Then closer to Leigh Sinton on the main Hereford to Worcester road they dominated, as they had for thousands of years, seemingly immovable objects, did it represent an impossible task?

On 22nd June, I met Adrian Hodges, a bowel surgeon recommended to me by Sami, my liver surgeon. I had asked to swap from the original bowel consultant, simply because the QE and the liver team had been so professional, this recommendation so far had the same positive feel and pace about it.

The appointment was at the Droitwich Spa Hospital where funnily enough, I had endured many consultations and physiotherapy in 2006, when I had my knee anterior cruciate ligament rebuild. It had changed somewhat, there was no sign of the knee clinic or the many signed and framed photos of famous sportsman that donned its walls, footballers, ballerinas, racing drivers all having gone to Droitwich all those years ago to have their knees looked at. Here I was again, in another hospital. I worked out to date, I had attended six different hospitals so far in this whole long process, perhaps I should have a stamp book and on the tenth hospital I get an award or free bed for a few nights at my leisure.

I had come from work on the train and Claudia met me there, after completing some brief paperwork with the receptionist, I was guided to a large waiting room along yet more medical corridors. Pretty much on time, Adrian appeared at the door, a tall man and announced my name looking hopefully around the room. I introduced myself and Claudia as we moved through the doorway and followed Adrian to his consultation room and two seats opposite his desk.

To be honest, I didn't know what to expect next, here I was having come along a long and winding road, having beaten every obstacle after obstacle with vigour, determination and a sense of survival. This guy could announce another twist, an evil turn from which I may be flawed or need to clamber back up, eventually finding my feet. How long would this go on for, how many more rounds of knockdowns would I take where I kept getting up smiling, coming through on my white steed of galloping positivity.

Adrian was an earnest kind of bloke, clearly an expert in his field and at times, very direct and serious. We started by him asking me to run through the whole story from the medical early in 2016, to the sigmoidoscopy discovery, the CT scan diagnosis of a bigger problem and then the subsequent treatments and operation. It took me a while, I went through in detail trying to get all of the medical terminology I had learnt through the experiences correct. With the odd question, Adrian examined my stomach and abdomen and we returned to our seats.

Drawing the simplest of pencil sketches, Adrian explained where he thought, from my historical medical notes, the cancer would be located, he hoped it should have been whacked by the same drugs that had worked so well on my liver but first, he needed to see it with his own eyes. Apparently, and I wasn't aware of this, the sigmoidoscopy I had undergone on my first diagnosis was not a full exploration of the bowel. I would need a colonoscopy, in essence, a full examination of the bowel. This would be different to the 'no anaesthetic approach' I had undergone with the sigmoidoscopy. I would need to be knocked out and whilst I would be breathing unassisted, I would effectively be unaware of the procedure. I was fine with this, the issue was if they found anything else, it would determine what procedure I underwent.

In some ways, the good news was that if it was just the Malverns, albeit the depleted Malverns smashed by our strategy to remove them with drugs, then keyhole surgery was an option, with an incision above the groin. They would take out the section affected by the cancer and stitch it back together. This would hopefully negate the need for a colostomy bag or diversion, my bowel should function normally post op. However, it would be a totally different ball game if I had more tumours in the unexplored section of the bowel or lower in the rectum. This could involve the surgery, creating a new opening for my number twos on the surface. *Great,* I thought, *a new arsehole, how novel.* I made some joke, but Adrian didn't laugh, he was being earnest again.

I asked if it went according to plan, would I have any do and don't post op. He replied that I would apparently be in for about four to five days and probably suffer from some wind initially. This time, my wife made a joke about that being fairly normal for me. Again, Adrian didn't crack a smile, he continued earnestly with his professional hat on. It was like being told off but as an adult for silly behaviour.

It reminded me of TJ's wedding where I was his best man. The wedding was in a Monmouthshire manor house, hired for the whole weekend. Some of us had bedrooms with stag heads on the walls and animal skin covers on the beds, other than the odd appearance of the owner, we were left to our own devices. After the ceremony, which was in the main reception room, a lavish meal and speeches followed which then turned into an evening of dancing and drinking. I can't remember what caused it but close friends, Fred and Chloe, were having a deep discussion, it looked serious, they took two chairs and sat 100 metres or so away from the house facing each other in heated discussion, under a couple of old apple trees.

A few of us helped ourselves each to another pint of Butty Bach from the barrel and pondered how we could assist. With plenty of suggestions and laughter, we settled on a plan. We decided upon a naked fly past, keeping in formation behind each other arms spread horizontally. Now, this would involve myself, Duncan (20 stone of Black Country blubber and a bit of muscle) and Jim (6 feet 5 inches of young 20 something prime specimen) stripping off somewhere secluded, running the 100 metres naked but pretending to be airplanes past the couple back to our safe landing strip.

"Whiskey Tango 10 to Whiskey Tango 20, Whiskey Tango 30, all checks completed, clear for take-off, follow my formation over!" I went first I had taken off my clothes, my tails, waistcoat, cravat and all other wedding gear and finally, hanging my socks and underpants on a peg in the medieval kitchen, opening the latched door and forming the shape of an airplane sprinted out into the evening air. Duncan followed the same procedure and then finally, Jim. I didn't stop but made my best airplane noise with my arms outstretched, as I circumnavigated the surprised couple who managed a startled smirk as I flew past. Duncan, behind me, was struggling to keep up, his rugby days long behind him, and he stopped next to the couple for a breather, leaning against the trunk of the apple tree, asking them if they had any water. Luckily, they saw the funny side and then to their amazement, Jim zoomed past close behind, making his best aircraft noise too 'meeeowwwww', he was now closing in on me.

Smirking from ear to ear, Jim and I lifted the latch to the kitchen, chatting feverishly about our successful mission. The problem was that the kitchen was now full of wedding guests tucking into generous helpings of leftovers. Jim and I nakedly stumbled in, too absorbed in conversation to notice until Jim's mum, Trish, looked at us in bewilderment, as though Jim and I had been having sex in the bushes and had kept our homosexual relationship a secret for years. As she let rip with a proper telling off, "Stanley Beavan, Jim…" Duncan burst through the door, panting and so out of breath, he failed to cover his manhood, again asking for water. I have not seen so many gaping mouths to this day, I think people thought we were three happy lovers of different sizes and this was the new free-way younger generations conducted themselves at weddings. It was too complicated to explain, and as adults, we were being told off. In the Droitwich consulting room, Adrian had the same serious look in his eye.

It was then that I tried adapting his sketch to show him where I thought the cancer was, and he suddenly roared with laughter, like I had cracked a hilarious joke. "If my job was as simple as relying on a patient's view of where the cancer was, it would make things a lot, lot easier!" he beamed. Adrian also made me realise I wasn't that young anymore, this could come back and they needed to see the results of the hospital analysis of the tumours to really get a handle on how aggressive this was and whether there were any genetic answers. I would have my colonoscopy on 3rd July, that wasn't far away.

I left the hospital consultation feeling this could go any way and I had limited control. I needed to adapt yet again, the balls were up in the air and there were no answers to so many questions. It takes a big step from a mind-set absorbing that sort of news to rescue a positive one. The drive home was a quiet one, so was the evening, my strong network of support was not in evidence no one phoned to see how it went. Perhaps people were bored of this repetitive medical treadmill now and quite frankly, I didn't blame them if they were, I would have to find positivity from somewhere else. I turned to writing this chapter, this was a start, thoughts still racing in my mind, the BOSE system in The Anaglypta Club blasting out an eclectic mix of songs as I wrote. As it happened, a song called *'Trip Switch'* was on by Nothing but Thieves—the key lyric 'What do we do when the lights go down?'

I pondered…*turn them back on, or light a candle??*

I had another focus too to distract me, a mate who had a military company providing high-end security in Hereford had suggested I act as a consultant to one of their companies, I started to explore how this would work, it was nice to switch off and think about something else.

I resolved that one day, I would move to the Malvern Hills, I felt strong. The next song that came over the speaker was

161

'Sledgehammer' by Peter Gabriel, at least the music seemed to be sending me a message. I would crack this nut one day.

Chapter 29
The Waiting

Having seen the bowel surgeon on 22nd June, I now had a colonoscopy planned. It was only two weeks away, if that, but here we were again, another obstacle another bit of the process. I didn't fear the procedure, I saw it as a good opportunity to get some sleep as I would be out cold. The bit that takes time to adjust to is the waiting, the waiting for news, this time, my concern was whether they would find more cancer in the bowel in addition to what they already knew about. A colonoscopy was a new thing, a more detailed investigative procedure and as CT scans/MRI scans wouldn't necessarily pick up everything in the bowel, this was going to be a key procedure which would determine my further treatment and how extreme my ultimate bowel surgery would be.

I was used to waiting, I had had to get used to it, throughout this journey, waiting a few days for results, sometimes weeks, sometimes waiting months to see if drugs had had any impact. I had trained my mind to cope and adapt to the waiting. I saw it as another challenge of my psyche, to overcome my weaknesses, impatience, any hint of panic, negative thoughts that would creep in as a result of waiting. There was very little 'what if' thinking, I would continue with my focuses and strategy like diet, in essence I would keep up the tight training regime until I had won the race. OK, so some will say that is just keeping busy but it's more than that. You really do have to channel positivity and be prepared for all eventualities whilst not letting it get to you. None of us know what is around the corner, literally none of us, I wasn't, therefore, any different. If it was bad news post-colonoscopy, I would deal with it in a positive way.

I had great people around me, who I adored…some tried to keep me focused with humour, Digger sending me his fancy dress photos as he got more and more leathered at a military do.

His text the next morning was even better '…just woken up on the kitchen floor…' (I could picture their kitchen and his realistic pirate costume which he would still be wearing, the parrot now wishing it had opted for a better life high up in the trees). 'I have no recollection of how I got home, I think I have broken my wrist!' (I thought for a moment what might have caused this, a cheeky attempt at a handstand to impress fellow revellers, I doubted that, or perhaps a wanking injury?)

'Gwen says I fucked up really, really badly and had to get dragged in from the yard outside by my mum after I told Gwen she was past it and was being put out to pasture. Apparently, there was a scuffle, I puked in someone's garden and was carried to a taxi'. (I now had second thoughts on what might have caused the wrist injury, a scuffle with the owner of the house, I know I would lamp some stranger who tried to puke in my garden or was it a scuffle with those trying to rescue him to the taxi…)

Digger continued, "All I know is my wrist hurts and my head is killing me." (I knew with a smile on my face what was coming next.)

'I am never going to drink again…!' (I fathomed, until next weekend at least anyway).

A few days later, I was sat having my lunchtime drink with Larry, the first time I had seen him in a while. Larry looked smarter, new polished shoes with jeans and a thin very trendy mac type three-quarter length coat. The temperature had dropped considerably following the unexpected heat wave, there was a hint of rain in the air. I was trying desperately to maintain my positivity in the face of more waiting, back to the start of another set of processes, starting with a full scan scheduled for the Friday. It is the unknown, what if thoughts that need to be driven from the mind.

Larry was telling me about his desire to dress a bit smarter now he had a more permanent woman and that marriage might be on the cards. I pondered this as I looked past my Becks Blue, out of the window and down to the canal below, as a barge trundled past, its carefree owner taking in the mass of concrete and brick structures towering around the waterway.

"How long have you been with her Larry?" I queried, smirking.

"Three weeks," was Larry's response.

Larry was having to take his time with this one, his patience for sexual adventure was already wearing thin, the pace was perhaps too slow. Larry explained that, at a recent office social, he had asked a fellow artist to tell him about her pussy, her response, "Nobody asks me about my pussy, Larry, it's fine, thank you!"

It made me smile but still my mind was adjusting to the next sequence of events, hospital Thursday to drink contrast dye, go to hospital Friday for more contrast dye and a more detailed chest, abdomen and pelvis scan, colonoscopy Monday. This would be followed by results for the scan and colonoscopy, I imagined, and then further on in that week, results from the genetic, hereditary analysis and within two weeks, the full results of the analysis of the tumour cells removed from my liver. Believe me, so many unknowns and possibilities that you can't start thinking 'what if'. You have to man up and wait it out despite that being extremely hard to do.

Thursday came and went, the dye was easy to down and the nurse who passed it to me, smiled as she said, "Just down it, it will light up your insides…" I imagined all my vital organs glowing in the dark. It reminded me of the stag do where I had been best man to TJ, my worst experience with glow in the dark resins. On returning to the B&B after a Friday night of revelling in Aberystwyth clubs, two fellow army officers pulled out of their bags 100 glow sticks, proceeded to snap them in half and flick the contents all over the dormitory where the 20 of us were sleeping. As I was saying authoritatively, in my best 'act not pissed' voice, "Come on, lads, this isn't our place, it's out of order," they let off all the foam fire extinguishers.

In a weird way, with the lights off, it was a surreal sight, a cross between an alien murder scene and Shrek having exploded after one too many doughnuts. The morning after, apart from a few piles of lingering foam and wet sections of carpet, the landlady seemed more content than I'd imagined, as the army captains/officers settled up for the used fire extinguishers in the most gentlemanly way possible. I did pity the next group to stay in that room when they turned off the lights, it would be a scene from the northern lights, green waves of fluorescent dye in a splattered pattern with spots across walls and ceiling. It had made me chuckle at the time, we were signed in under a false group name the 'Mufftree Ramblers'!

On Friday, 30th June, I had found myself sat in the X-Ray /CT department of a Birmingham private hospital waiting room, in a surgical gown and dressing gown with my clothes and belongings in a Tesco-style shopping basket. Around me were six other people all sat in their gowns, baskets at their feet. Each of us instructed to drink a different concoction of contrast dyes to light up our insides. I wondered about each of these individuals, their stories, their lives, their illnesses. Before being ill, I was oblivious to people experiencing these sorts of things and ignorant of the good work done by the people working in the medical profession. These were beautiful people and experiencing a major turn in an otherwise normal life. Some were drinking a thick white substance by the jug full, I was glad mine seemed more like water apart from the medicine like taste.

The scan room was staffed by two Asian nurses, both respectfully dressed in their cultural headscarves. We exchanged chitchat as the more chatty of the two got on with the insertion of the cannula to administer the additional contrast dye. No pain, I knew to keep my arm perfectly straight as I clenched and unclenched my fist, the tourniquet helping to flush out the veins.

I followed the breathing instructions from the automated scanner voice, as I hardly felt the contrast dye fill my bloodstream on the third trip through the CT scanner. I remember thinking, if I have an erection now, would these two nurses hiding behind their glass screen be impressed, my penis glowing on the screen in front of them. It was over quickly (I mean the scan not the erection), I had got dressed and collected a package of laxatives from reception in advance of the scan on Monday. I would not be able to eat fibrous foods all weekend and would need to starve myself for 24 hours prior to the colonoscopy whilst pumping my body full of laxatives. Happy days!

How was I doing mentally, I wondered. I concluded I was still positive but would really have to wait until the end of all of these processes, not knowing when that would be or what outcomes to eventually expect.

The next day, I had an instruction from Digger on the phone regarding the forthcoming colonoscopy, to look out for a rare bottle top he claimed to have force fed me the night I dropped him into an ice cold bath a few years back. What bottle top? I had no recollection of it but didn't put it past him. In essence, he was asking for it back, that was after we had sifted it from the other long lost items like Lego bricks, coins, lumpy indigestible bits of my wife's cooking. I imagined that we could wash it first, sterilise it and post it to him. You can always rely on your friends to cheer you up at low points during the waiting game, most of them anyway.

The Saturday before my colonoscopy, I went for a run with my son, Flynn. It was the first run for a long time and it felt good. It was almost six weeks since the liver operation and being in intensive care. Disappointingly, he beat me by a long way but I seriously thought at the time, I will beat him in the not too distant future.

Chapter 30
A Turn in the Road

The 3rd July was a bright sunny day, my wife drove my car with me in the passenger seat via Worcester to the private hospital in Birmingham. My mind had been racing the last few days, not negatively but this was a key phase. The secondary cancer they had hopefully extracted from my liver, the bowel cancer, the primary cancer was still unchecked and the possibilities were endless. The best case scenario I understood to be cutting out a section of bowel where the cancer was, the worst case scenario multiple sections of bowel removed and a new arsehole!

I probably pissed a few people off over the last few days on text or removing them from my mind, I needed to focus with as much effort as possible and be ready to absorb whatever was thrown at me.

As expected, I was ushered to a private room and I was thankful that the bowel surgeon had squeezed me in before his two week annual holiday. It was a pleasant room I surveyed, as the porter ushered us in, the sun was streaming through the window. After texting for a bit, I was visited by someone from the restaurant to choose my post-operation sandwich, then by another nurse suggesting I got kitted out ready for operation, in my hospital pants, stockings and surgical gown, still occasionally visiting the en suite to empty my bowels, not that there was anything left in there. I was starving hungry, I hadn't eaten since 9:00 a.m. the previous morning. I bored myself of texting, had read the paper and after a visit from the admission nurse, fell asleep on the bed, trying to slow the pace of my mind down.

I woke up when a couple more nurses arrived, more questions and form filling. I was wrist banded and was then pretty much ready to go. I eventually had a theatre nurse arrive to walk me to theatre. It felt familiar, as my eyes watched various nurses darting from room to room and some poor bloke coming back from theatre with multiple tubes sticking out of him. That had been me six weeks ago, I was relieved I was walking completely normally down the corridor.

Walking through the start of the theatre ward, was weird, in the past, I would have been on a bed being wheeled by chatty porters, this time I took more in being upright, a cold gust of very pure air hitting me as we moved through the double doors. Everywhere looked sterile, as we moved through two more doors and we were then suddenly in the small pre-op room, a bed and six or seven theatre team guys stood around it. They were all waiting for me and introduced themselves as we each shook hands. It was more like a client networking event for a moment or being introduced to a group of your mates' friends down the pub, one guy had the most amazing curly moustache too, I thought he might start singing 'Go Compare' at any moment. I got on the bed and then more questions, full name? Date of birth? Had I any piercings? Caps on my teeth? Was I allergic to anything? Whilst curly moustache asked away, on the other side of me, the anaesthetist proceeded to insert a cannula into the back of my left wrist and another was asking me about the weekend and if I had had a BBQ? These guys were in a slick rhythm and doing things all at once but not interfering with one another, it was very professional.

The last I remember was the anaesthetist injecting into the cannula, then a cold sensation spreading half way up my left arm, I was challenging myself, trying to fight it by talking away and looking at the clock. All very painless and then I was awake in recovery, a nice chap from the theatre team again guarding over me. I felt pretty good really quickly and started chatting to him. I can't actually remember the detail but I was asking him how long he had been working in theatre and whether it had all gone well. As I was speaking, I looked to my left and the bowel surgeon Adrian was standing there. In his surgical blue gown, his face mask lowered around his neck. After the civilities, he told me he had just been to see my wife and to tell her about the procedure. Then he launched into it.

"Well, Stanley, we are in unchartered territory to a large degree, not unheard of but very rare," he paused, "there is absolutely no sign of the cancer, no scar tissue, marks, or anything at all. I made several runs up and down your colon looking out for anything but it has gone completely. I can only assume the treatment and strategy in your case has totally destroyed any sign of it." Taking a moment to look me directly in the eyes and lean in closer over the metal side of my bed, he continued, "I had a word with the liver team regarding your results from your liver laboratory studies too and there was no trace of cancer in the tumours/scar tissue they removed either." Adrian smiled, "Again this is very rare. This poses us with a dilemma, Stanley," he breathed in slowly, deep in thought, "do we take out the section of bowel where it had been? Or do we do nothing and continue to monitor things?"

I thought for a second or two and said without hesitation, "You're the expert, you decide!"

"OK, I want to get the results of the scan on Friday and check your CEA score, then I want to book you in for a PET scan. I also want to discuss you with my group of surgeons to agree a strategy." He again took time to inhale slowly, then again smiled, "It is a nice dilemma to have!" with that, we chatted a bit about my strategy having worked so well and we shook hands and Adrian was gone, leaving me to absorb this latest turn in the road.

I wasn't jumping up and down, there were still tests to come back and a major bowel operation was still a distinct possibility but the overall feel here was positive, no new cancer had been found and the existing aggressive cancer that had spread to the bowel had done a runner. I was getting closer to a resolution, I felt it in my bones but still so many variables. What if, for example, the CT scan showed cancer back in the liver or some other organ where it was a more difficult surgery option all together, or my CEA scan was back up to an abnormal level? I would deal with it, right then I was feeling good.

As we drove out of Birmingham, Claudia at the wheel, I wrestled with telling people where I now found myself but opted to keep the news under wraps until it was either certain or I knew more about whether there was a new operation phase. There were certain people I wanted to tell but resigned myself not to, despite knowing they wanted updates and cared. I ignored several texts, from inquisitive people I loved.

Chapter 31
The Dream

That night I had a vivid dream…

I was on one side of a wooded canal, on the other I was glimpsing, through the tall oaks and ash trees, the light green of wheat waving gently in the wind and there it was, the most beautiful hare sat upright directly opposite me. I watched its muscular frame, privileged to watch such a handsome creature so close, it knew I was there. With the most amazing acceleration, it took off running parallel to the canal along the edge of the wheat field, gaining speed. I had burst into a run myself catching sight of it through gaps in the leafy vegetation, then it was gone. I ran further, the trees petering out to give me a direct view of the wheat field and there, as I stopped for breath, was something else, a beautiful brown with a lightness to its coat but an air of dangerous cruel intent as it stalked the path on which the hare would have run. It was powerful to the rear, its huge hind legs almost higher and more muscular than its front legs, its long nose down on the ground its ears seemingly pinned backwards.

I was nervous now, this was a lot bigger than I imagined a wolf to be, a powerhouse of hunting prowess. I tried not to make a sound but I was still breathing hard after the sprint along the bank and then with its nose sensing something in the air, it turned, its evil eyes focusing on me, its frame turning towards me, its posture like a cat getting ready to stalk a young rabbit blissfully unaware. With no more than a split second, it was moving quickly to a narrow section of canal blocked by years of neglect, stumps and branches clogging the watercourse. It was in the air now, leaping forward and then across the canal, running onto the bank and towards me.

Before I could react, it was within 10 metres, it slowed and was circling me, its growling mouth dropping saliva onto the grass, pure evil ready to devour me in a painful enduring execution of its prey. It was getting closer as it circled, I could smell it, its long nose and fangs pointing towards me guiding it nearer, its eyes never leaving me, there was no pity in those eyes. I decided to act.

I reacted first running towards it, catching its attention in total surprise for a split second, I roared as loud as I could and as it altered its posture, not sure whether to fight or flight, I kicked towards it, scuffing its hindquarters as it turned, growling. I ran towards it again making a huge noise, making myself as big as possible with my arms, it looked as though it would attack this time but I ran straight for it. With a degree of reluctance, it was having second thoughts and adopted a more retreating sideways motion, eventually breaking into a run. I had won this battle as the devil-like beast, ran into the distance and out of sight.

Chapter 32
The Tide Had Turned

I didn't feel a rush of euphoria after my discharge from hospital, it was positive stuff but a lot to take in and I didn't want to get too optimistic while there were so many unanswered questions and more tests to be done. I felt exhausted mentally suddenly, perhaps I was still feeling the effects of the starvation, laxative and anaesthetic. I doubted that. This was like a numbness in my brain, a data overload, like I had achieved a major goal and then nothingness. I wanted to be on my own, I didn't immediately turn to those who were there for me, I needed time to absorb and think, compartmentalise this whole new episode. There were so many possible outcomes there could have been and yet this was looking exceedingly positive.

I had been watching a film when my mobile showed a missed call and then a message from Adrian, my bowel surgeon. I had been annoyed, I had switched it to silent, I now wanted to speak to Adrian more than watch the film, his message did, however, promise to ring back later or the following day. I turned the volume on the ringer up high on the phone and carried on watching 'The Line' an action film. When the phone rang, I had hit pause on the movie like something possessed and sprinted for the kitchen table where the phone was sat, for a better signal, knowing instantly that it was Adrian.

Adrian was polite enquiring firstly if it was Stanley...

"Yes!" I had replied!

"So I now have had the opportunity to review the CT scan results you had on Friday, and there are no nodes or signs of anything on the liver." There was a pause, "I want to book you in for a Positron Emission Tomography scan (PET) which is a metabolic scan, repeat an MRI scan on the liver and pelvis," he again paused, taking a more definite tone. "Now, if I was a betting man, I suspect all of those scans will come back negative, which means we have a decision to make in terms of the section of bowel where the cancer had been, this is very much unchartered waters, and it means that clinically and pathologically, you will have had a complete response!"

I wondered what pathological meant and told myself I would look it up immediately after coming off the phone. Adrian went on, "I have spoken to a few experts about you, one oncologist said if it was him he would take out that bit of bowel just as a precaution, another wanted to think about it. Overall, this is Good News Stanley, you are doing extremely well, let's get the scans booked in and that might help us reach a decision, speak to my secretary, Maddy, while I am away and get these booked in." I had thanked Adrian and was again left in utter mind-bending numbness. I was achieving goals, heading in the right direction, the overall strategy was working 100%. I didn't say much that evening on text or to my wife, I needed to process this carefully. It was easy to overact when I had more tests to come and possibly another major surgical procedure.

The one thing I did do, as I sat blankly looking at my phone was text my oncologist Tom, saying, "I need to chat to you, have news, decision needed."

The next morning, 5th July, Tom called me apologising for not picking up the text from 10 p.m. the previous evening. I could forgive that, these guys worked ruthlessly hard. I took time explaining the scenario to Tom, I had made notes the previous evening and used them to relay some of the medical terms to Tom correctly and set out the direction things were headed and the possible dilemma looming. Interestingly, Tom talked through various considerations concluding that he would opt for no operation and regular monitoring. So two oncologists, two different views but these were more positive conversations to have with these guys, they were no longer sombre, but more upbeat, I was an interesting conundrum for them to consider, something out of the norm, unusual.

If I was honest, I felt more inclined not to have the operation, I felt fine but I was no expert on microscopic cells that given the vicious nature of the cancer originally reported, could kill me.

I felt the tide was turning in my favour, first the secondary cancer smashed and now the primary had apparently done a runner, starved of its nutrients, blasted by the right measure and type of medicine and a huge dose of positive vibes.

I often retreated to my man cave, hitting my Lenovo tablet each evening, trying to extract the chronological sequence of events and what I was going through. I bluetoothed Spotify from my S7 edge to the BOSE speaker and would hit the volume, playing shuffle through my song list and started writing chapters in this book. The more I wrote, the more cathartic the process seemed to be, I started finding that the writing was connecting better with my brain and getting out all that was impacting me. Always at my feet, Skyla, my two-year-old Working Cocker, sprawled out on her side, dreaming about tennis balls but always faithfully ready for the next command. This whole process, from the general company medical where a suggestion to seek further investigation was made by Dr Vegas, to this point in time, now near on 12 months. There were more scans, new processes, possible operations looming on the horizon. I told myself keep going, you are nearly there, take your mind off things, focus on something else. Don't analyse, look forward only. I was so busy at work, it helped massively as a distraction, we had a raft of new business and clients to set up.

Chapter 33
PET Scan, Tuesday, 11 July

It had been a wetter July day, a break from the roasting sunshine which had basked the Midlands for seemingly weeks on end. I had been booked in for a PET scan following on from the colonoscopy the previous week and had an awareness that a PET scan was pretty much as detailed as scans get. Other than that, I was not really familiar with how it differed to a CT scan. I wasn't nervous I knew there would be an injection a bit like the contrast dye for the CT scan but this one was apparently radioactive. The woman who phoned me to book me in at the QE's PET scanning department, told me not to do any exercise beforehand, not to eat four hours before and to expect an injection an hour before the scan, where I would be left in a room for an hour on my own. Eight hours after the scan I was not allowed near pregnant women! Christ, I began wondering, what was in these injections?

On arrival, I had been signed in and immediately told there was an hour delay, so my plan to get there early and be seen quickly had failed. A 3:30 p.m. arrival became a 4:30 p.m., then a 5:30 p.m. before I was ushered into a small room with a bed at one end. This was even before my hour of waiting for the injection to circulate had begun.

The male nurse was impressed with my veins and quickly pounced on a nice juicy one on my right arm, inserting a cannula without much pain caused. He proceeded to tell me that the contents of the injection arrived in a vile protected by a lead case. This really was radioactive powerful stuff. I didn't feel the injection running through my veins but after the nurse had left me for my hour and I had turned Spotify on my phone, listening to a great play list compiled by a mate, my jaw started to ache. In fact, all my teeth began to ache, albeit my eyes were heavy and ready to think about sleep. After about 40 minutes, a female nurse guided me to the loo, in order for me to empty my bladder.

I duly did this, politely informing her when I came out, that the loo was in danger of flooding. Not because of me but someone else had tried to set a new world record for the amount of toilet paper that can be shoved down a loo. I spent another ten minutes in the room, trying to keep relaxed and listening to the cool vibes of the play list. I loved the fact someone had passed this set of tunes onto me, it made me feel positive.

The scanner room was similar to a CT scanner, the equipment looked the same and I had to drop my trousers to my knees for this one and put my hands high above my head as though I was reaching out for something on tiptoe. Like so many times before, the staff retreated to the safe haven of the adjoining room, peering out from behind their glass screen. There was a bit of a buzz from the scanner as it ratcheted up its power, I watched digital numbers on the side of the scanner increasing and decreasing in a seemingly irregular order, I had no idea what they meant. I wondered as I lay there how much damage these numerous scans were doing to me, essential but sending rays through my body.

The scan itself was only 20 minutes, I hitched up my trousers, and was glad to leave after three and half hours of PET scan department hospitality. As I drove myself home, I pondered how the results from this scan would fare, I felt so close to final answers after a year of maximising my strategy, fighting the cause and delivering on the bits I could do, having pushed the medical aspects as hard as I could. The fight wasn't over but I wasn't on chemo, I had been lucky, an inoperative liver was now fully functioning post-operation and the primary cancer was nowhere to be seen. These were brilliant signs for me, I couldn't have asked for more, I felt numb and yet apprehensive that either this PET scan or seeing the liver consultant the next day would throw up something new or an off track twist or turn for the worse. It wasn't that I felt negative, I didn't but I had done everything I could do, it was a case of just waiting.

I had been robust throughout the year and now I was almost twiddling my thumbs waiting for the outcomes, I felt suddenly more emotional. I was so pleased I was now where I was but I found it harder to express it or articulate what I was experiencing. Certain people I was trying to avoid on the phone or found it difficult to talk to. I knew how dire this set of circumstances could be, the other side of the spectrum, my chips at the casino of life were so far landing me big wins but it felt like I was still putting all my chips on one colour waiting to see if it landed when the roulette wheel stopped spinning. I felt like it was psychologically harder to breathe sometimes and I had little patience for some situations either at work or personally. In some ways, I already felt like I wanted to celebrate but there was so much more to come, wait for and it was post effort news, it was after the fight after the surgical procedures, this was it.

I hoped that the PET scan results would at least be available for Sami, when he sat down with me the following day to run through my results seven weeks post operation. Literally, as I thought that, his secretary Amy texted me, she was preparing Sami's notes for the outpatient appointment with me and wanted to know if I had had the PET scan. I was really impressed with her dedication, proactivity and at 8 p.m., was working hard to now get the results of the PET scan I had just come from, so Sami could give me a full overview.

This was it, crunch time and a full breakdown the next day from one of the best liver surgeons. There was no hiding from it, a bit more waiting and I would soon know. I channelled any emotion I was experiencing and looked for the positives. I was looking forward to seeing Sami, I respected him and what he had done for me, he was at the top of his game and his skill set had potentially saved my life. I also focused on the fact I felt great and ready for anything.

Chapter 34
Against the Odds

My meeting with Sami was on 12th July at the consultation suites of the private hospital in Birmingham, it was a beautiful period building with almost Turkish style stain glass windows, allowing distorted sun light to flood into the waiting room as my wife and I waited to catch up with Sami. When he came to get us, we exchanged big grins like old friends, Sami was about my age, good-looking and very relaxed.

Once in the consultation room, we initially exchanged pleasantries and he asked to see the wound and how it was heeling. I took off my jacket, undid my shirt and made for the treatment couch, taking off the dressing as I did so. Sami could see the over granulation and then proceeded to burn it off using what looked like a joss stick. It was, in fact a stick of silver nitrate. It stung a bit as he applied the end to the tumour-like over granulated flesh, it turned a blackish grey as it was singed. Some of the silver nitrate dribbled from the wound mixing with fluid and running in a line down my side and onto my hand. I didn't mind at the time, I was getting another part of the process done. The exercise with silver nitrate didn't take long, I was back in the chair facing Sami across his desk in no time at all, a slight stinging feeling where my flesh had been burnt off.

Sami took no time to then tell me that my liver was now normal size and apart from a few pockets of fluid which would dissipate, the scan showed everything was normal, no residual or recurrent tumour or abnormalities. It was literally like hearing sweet music to my ears.

This was already a massive relief but I wasn't jumping up and down. Sami went on, "There were no viable tumour cells identified in any of the specimens taken from your liver during the operation, only cancer deposits, in effect the treatment has completely destroyed the cancer, which is in keeping with a complete pathological response to chemotherapy."

Initially, my reaction was one of disappointment, I had wanted to know more about it, cell types etc. and had hoped the lab at the QE would have a lot to say about it. "In addition," Sami continued, "the PET scan in relation to the liver has not shown anything either of concern, of course you need Adrian to comment on the bowel section but as far as I am concerned and subject to the final MRI scan, you are cured."

As I thought about this major statement, probably one of the most important statements I had ever received or heard through my ears in 45 years, Sami said something strange, "I have only ever seen this in six or seven patients." He was referring to my complete response, the fact that no cancer cells had been found, not one, the fact everything had been destroyed.

"Over what period and in how many patients?" I asked after a pause, still absorbing these huge facts about my life, my survival, my future as a human.

"Over a five year period, that is about 1,250 patients!" he said smiling very calmly.

I nearly fell off my chair, so did my wife who was busy taking notes. I had to double check I had heard this correctly, I was blown away, Claudia was the same asking the same question in a different way, "So statistically, you have only seen that in 0.5% of patients?" she asked, her mathematical brain working better than mine at that point.

"Yes," Sami responded, smiling. It was the reality, this was a rare thing, a total response to the treatment, strategy adopted. My mind was at this point saying to me, 'What the fuck is going on?'

Sami explained that subject to what Adrian came back with, in respect of his part of the PET scan and pelvis MRI scan, it may just be a case then of monitoring me at six monthly intervals moving forward. Sami agreed with my emerging view as we talked, that there was no point in having a bowel operation for the sake of it, if there was no detectable cancer, he reiterated that I would be getting regular monitoring for two years from now, as in a third of patients reoccurrence happens. I would only be back to normal population risk levels after five years. I would, however, need Adrian and my oncologist to agree.

I felt so close now to resolution. I left the consultation suite again numb, positive that I had turned yet another massive corner but still a few weeks away from a full statement on the status of my illness from all experts. I needed Adrian to come back to me and for that, I would have to wait until I was through the MRI scans.

I had been off alcohol for the whole year and had asked Sami four times if it was OK to drink, now my liver was back to normal. "You can do whatever," was his response, although he had given an advisory, 'in moderation' type caveat.

I said goodbye to Claudia dropping her at the QE, so she could catch the train back to Hereford from the university train station, I then drove back to the office.

I sat at my desk with so many things going around in my head, I felt like my head was going to burst and I felt waves of emotion rising up within me. I decided I needed to talk and grabbing one of those that had been there for me, went to a nearby bar for a beer. I sat in the beer garden with a pint of fosters and drank it with a tear in my eye, I loved the taste and had waited so long for a real beer. I got some of what I had just been through out of my system, the odds of this happening had been 0.5%. A miracle, it definitely felt like it.

That week, I had lunch with a few other friends who had been there for me during the process. I downloaded to them which was cathartic and felt good. I drank a glass of wine on the Thursday and on the Friday bought champagne for my team, then having a much looked forward to glass of Rioja with another good friend who I owed lunch to. Tina had lost her father to cancer and had been a strong supporter through the process. Over lunch, she explained that her friend had been diagnosed with cancer at the same time as me and the same type bowel spread to the liver. Unfortunately, her battle of life had not been as successful and she had sadly passed away. I was shocked and again numb. I had had a response, a full response, this person hadn't experienced the same, cancer seemed a cruel uncompromising evil, seemingly selecting at random and dishing out different experiences.

I was kind of celebrating where I was, whilst not there completely I had to take stock of where I was and what had been achieved. People wanted to know, wanted to be part of the

181

journey. I had to take the positives while they lasted, tomorrow could be very different.

Over the weekend, I found myself repeating the sequence of events to close friends, met with sometimes disbelief, sometimes tears and just smiles, hugs and positivity. I loved it, I started feeling stronger, people were my tonic for feeling good, at that moment this was a great wave to ride and I felt like it was going to be a positive outcome even if I did need another operation on the bowel. We would have to wait and see but here I was, defying the odds, smashing it!

I thought back to my earlier life, taking risks on top of cars, or risks with friends like Digger where we had diced with death and come out unscathed, almost proud of having cheated the bad outcomes, drawing on the massive wave of positives, a rush of adrenaline. It felt the same, I was running again with death as an outcome but was beating it, not fearing death, just respecting it and managing to outwit it. That sounds cocky but that is what this felt like. I was a maverick, a risk taker, this was nothing new, my past had helped me put this into a chilled perspective and with the right mind-set and approach, you give yourself the best opportunity. I had flipped a switch early on in this process and applied it. The same switch I had flipped at different times in my life.

I spoke to TJ on the Thursday, telling him about the news regarding the liver. I could confide in TJ about the emotional element, feeling like I was coming out of a fight where death was a reality. TJ and I talked about his first tour of Afghanistan, as a bomb operator licensed to diffuse Improvised Explosive Devices on the battlefield, this was a high-risk job and TJ had to get everything right. The four people doing the job before him had been killed, the reality of death had been there in Afghan, TJ had to be on his game to outwit it, to maximise the bits of the process he could deliver on. We had gone skiing just before his Afghanistan tour, to Bulgaria, a lads' trip, drinking, skiing off-piste in avalanche areas and doing black runs and slopes closed due to health and safety. We knew TJ might not come back from the Afghan tour, the odds were highly stacked, a real risk of being killed. We remembered those times and then TJ talked about coming home, the numbness, the emotion of having survived, having avoided death. It was what I was going through now a kind of post-traumatic stress. TJ had struggled with people, looking at them differently on his return, they (and me included) had not understood what he was experiencing. I did now, I got it, I could see exactly his perspective, you are thrown into deep waters, cold and dark and you have to tread water, keeping your chin up. TJ had done another tour since then and had come through it, bouncing back, I needed to do the same, get the right perspective and channel the emotion. I just needed the final pieces of the jigsaw.

My boys were relaxed as ever, we had deliberately kept things calm throughout the year, normal as possible. Yes, they had seen my with a cannula in my arm sat in an armchair at home and Josh had shed a few tears the first time I had gone into hospital but other than that, they had not visited me in hospital, seen me in any other circumstances than near enough normal. OK, so I had lost my hair and there had been physical changes, but again, I wore them with pride and purpose, the impact on them was as minimal as possible.

So when Claudia decided late on the evening of having seen the liver surgeon, to give them a low down as they sat on the sofa on my latest good news, they didn't even jump up and down, I think we got an 'OK, good' and a grunt of acknowledgement. Claudia was flummoxed by their reaction. However, on reflection, she decided it was a good thing, the kids weren't emotional or shocked, they were seeing no difference to me as it was, to them this was a relaxed process and they didn't need to get excited. It meant we had actually protected them very well from this, their school reports were fantastic and they were happy. Claudia eventually saw this, let them just carry on, it was one less thing to worry about.

I was emerging from this battle and now I wanted to be there for the people who had been there for me. Having lunch and drinks with people that week, I realised how many of my friends had issues going on in their lives. I wanted to offer to be there for them like they had been there for me. As I had walked out of the office that evening, Julie had been stood waiting for a lift, she looked tearful. She had been someone who had come to see me at home during chemo and had regularly sent me messages, enquiring after my well-being. It had all been a boost for me helping with the positivity.

Now, it was my turn, as I looked her in the eye and asked, "Is everything OK?"

As she was bursting into tears, I gave her a hug and asked if she wanted a chat. This was down to a bloke and I gave my view on what I would do, explaining how different blokes were to women in their approach. I offered to be there for any further advice. My last words to Julie were 'chin up!' something that I had been told regularly which I made myself do.

That weekend, we had been at a BBQ with close friends, Deano, Jane, Fred and Chloe. After a great meal, we had all been lying on our backs on a rug on the lawn, staring up on the perfectly still, clear star filled night sky. It was mesmerising, everyone was happy for me, we had just all watched 30 years of the six of us having great fun times in a photo montage/compilation on the TV, a lovely gesture by Deano and Jane. The stars were so amazing but I knew somewhere up there was something very powerful. I couldn't say it was religion based, faith based but I felt power that the cosmos, the universe was in control and had helped me here. I had spoken to it on occasion, asking for things and felt energy, it had if nothing else given me self-belief and positivity. Against all the odds, I was moving forward and I loved this universe, I felt alive. We were all silent for a while just staring up at that star filled sky, all happy, I felt the energy of friends happy for me, I felt the power, I felt I could achieve anything.

Chapter 35
One Year On, 21 July

21st July was a dull day, raining pretty much from daybreak, putting a stop to the warm summer sun that had been a constant pleasantry for quite some time. I felt a little jaded, the night had been a late one, an all office drinks and canapés to welcome some London colleagues to the Midlands. Whilst I had chosen to drink only non-alcoholic beers until 9 p.m., I had then drunk three pints of lager. I would have been fine, however I was requested to be nil by mouth from 2 a.m. in advance of the 8:30 a.m. MRI scan appointment at the private hospital. I had stopped drinking at 12:30 a.m. but had wanted to get one of my female mates a taxi, given she was suffering the effects of too much wine. She had been there as a mate over the last year and I would repay the favour, as with any mate that had been there for me, whenever I could. I managed to get her in a taxi at 12:45 a.m., texted her to check she was in through her front door and then tried to get sleep before the early start.

I felt jaded as a result of all of the above but I was otherwise positive. I had something medical to do again, I would maximise my performance in the scanner, making sure I followed instructions precisely, lying as still as possible, holding my breath as instructed and making sure I did everything to give the best scans of my liver and pelvis. I was also looking forward to the fact this was the last treatment I was aware of. It would then be a case of my bowel surgeon, Adrian, delivering my results and whether another operation was required, whether on the PET scan or this MRI scan they had detected any signs of the primary cancer or any other cancer for that matter. More waiting but I was getting so close to resolution, so close to outcomes.

On arrival at the hospital, I was directed to a small outbuilding which was signposted MRI unit. It was a small building and as I entered, seemed to comprise five main sections, the scanner on the left of the entrance, a small reception room and scanner control room in the middle, a waiting room and two small changing rooms to the right hand side. After introducing myself to the jolly receptionist, I was given a clipboard with a standard health questionnaire, things like had I metal fragments in my eyes? I was tempted to put, 'fuck no, but that sounds painful!' and ask, 'what activity has a risk of metal fragments in the eyes…?' I pondered that as I completed and signed the questionnaire and also the form confirming my personal details. I suddenly thought…dropping your glasses in a liquidiser!

After handing in the forms, I was asked to change into a surgical gown, keeping my underpants and socks on and to put my belongings in a small locker, handing the key to the radiologist. I then sat in the waiting room reading 'Hello' magazine, checking out Prince Harry's American girlfriend. The woman opposite me was waiting for her husband who was having his first ever scan. She was nervous for him and I tried to instil some positivity, assuring her that, apart from being a tight fit, the process was otherwise just a bit noisy. I felt like an old hand at this now forgetting how many scans I had actually been for. I did, however, remember I was apprehensive on my first one too.

It was my turn and I was ushered in by the radiologist, a small guy possibly Polish, in his early 60s I estimated. It was just him as he got me lying down on the scanner bed, explaining the procedure to first scan my pelvis and then circa an hour later my liver. As he peered over his glasses and smartly trimmed moustache, I would in his words, "Be here for a while!" The scanner looked like any other, this one a Siemens, a creamy beige colour with numerous dials and buttons either side of the tunnel looming beyond my feet. I was given head phones to listen to the radio and asked to choose a station, I picked radio 2, Chris Evans suddenly chirping away in my ears, with far too much energy for 8:30 a.m. on a Friday morning.

The radiologist positioned the panels over my pelvis, strapped my arms and hands pretty much to my sides and then disappeared into the control room to begin the first scan. Intermittently, I then heard my new Polish friend through my headphones pre-warning me when the bed would be moving and when each scan would start. It is hard remaining perfectly still, for me I managed to get a dead arm and a numb arse cheek, either it was the prolonged stillness or Chris Evans was sending parts of my body to sleep as he interviewed Nadia of 'The Bake Off' about her new book. It felt like ages before I emerged from the tunnel, well everything below my neck, my head had been just outside the scanner as it was a pelvis scan.

It was now time for the liver scan, this would require an injection. I had a conversation as to which arm the radiologist would prefer and he said he didn't mind so we opted for my left arm. Within seconds, he had tourniqueted my upper arm, made me clench my fist and located a nice vein, and whilst asking me to turn my arm slightly inwards, inserted the needle with ease, painless as I looked the other way, pinching the back of my neck with my other hand, a seemingly customary way of controlling the pain for me now. There was, however, no need.

After another discussion over what was going to happen over the next hour, I was again left listening to Chris Evans and the Beautiful South as the radiologist disappeared into the control room and told me through the head phones the bed was about to move, with that I moved slowly into the tunnel this time my head fully in the tube. It was tight, I pitied a large person they would have to put Vaseline on the sides to get them in and more importantly back out again. I wondered if the fire brigade needed to be called ever to anyone stuck in the scanner, smoke billowing from the motor for the moving parts of the bed, it having burnt out, unable to haul the load of human mass stuck in the tube.

This time, I was given instructions to hold my breath, I was used to this but I didn't get much warning, literally, 'take a breath in' and the scanner would start its electronic musical of dull notes sometimes a pattern on low thrumps or high shrill bleeps. It was sometimes 20 seconds I held my breath for, I counted in my head, quite tricky when you are lying as still as possible and after not eating or drinking for over seven hours. I regretted letting rip in the tunnel, whilst in the comfort of the knowledge that my controller was in a different room, the gaseous emission had nowhere to escape to and attempted to hamper my breathe holding. I prayed that, in 30 minutes when my new buddy came to release me from my toilet roll like hiding place, the smell would have dissipated.

I didn't feel the dye go in at all, I just hoped it was giving the radiologist a clear picture, so that we could accurately identify any suspicious areas. I hoped, in my heart, that the good news would continue and that nothing would be found. I was realistic that, whatever the outcome, it would be a few days yet where I would need to be patient again, ready for good or bad news. I was used to the waiting but thoughts were going through my head now, what if they don't find anything, is this my last scan for a while, no more operations. I tried to steer my mind away from such thoughts. I focused on how surreal it was, listening to radio 2 whilst having particles of goodness knows what zooming through my body at mind-blowing speeds.

I was starving when I came out of the scanner, my needle was taken out, I got dressed and was driving away from the hospital in no time at all, turning into the nearest McDonalds and ordering a quarter pounder with cheese meal. Completely off my diet plan but I didn't care, I felt like I was on the road to a positive outcome, I felt good.

Chapter 36
Finality

Monday, 24th July had been one of those days that challenges your positivity. Firstly, I had chased the bowel surgeon's secretary to ask him to contact me, only to be told he was again in theatre. I was being as patient as I could be but it had now been two weeks since the PET scan and I needed to know about the bowel; the liver I had the low down, I was happy. The process I had dreamed about completing was so close now to an outcome. The bowel was the missing segment.

That evening, I still had heard nothing, despite having phoned the secretary earlier, it worried me as the bowel surgeon was due to fly off again on holiday shortly. As I drove out of the city on my homeward journey, the day seemingly got worse with the dashboard computer showing that I now had a complete puncture to the passenger offside and the front driver side was also losing pressure. This wasn't the first time I had driven from the work car park with punctures and whilst I had run flat tyres, this didn't look good. The bonus with run flats is you can keep driving at 50mph albeit it isn't always easy and in this case, the back of the car was snaking occasionally, especially if I braked. I had jumped out to take a look and could see tacks in both tyres. *Oh well, it's only money,* I thought, knowing full well these tyres aren't cheap, 450 for a pair. It looked like I would be needing two of the buggers. I was determined to go back to Pirelli this next time, Goodyear F1 Asymmetrics seemed cursed for me.

The next day, I was sat at my desk working, when I saw the QE number flash up on my mobile screen, I managed to get it in time. I couldn't actually have missed the sound either, I had put it on full volume with the hope the surgeon would call, so everyone in the office heard the ring. It was Adrian, the surgeon, asking if it was convenient to talk. I politely asked him to give me a moment while I grabbed a pad and pen and diverted quietly to a meeting room for privacy.

"Fire away," I motioned, once sat in a meeting room chair, ready with my pen.

"So as you know," Adrian started his commentary, "the CT scan showed no further issues, your colonoscopy showed no abnormalities either and I have now had the chance to review the PET scan with the doctor from that department which also shows nothing further in your liver or your bowel." I was already relieved, I knew the PET scan was a very detailed overview. Adrian continued, "The MRI scan of your liver showed no further lesions and the MRI of your bowel showed no residual tumour or new nodes. It is a Complete Response to chemotherapy treatment and as you know, very rare and as you also know, it leaves a dilemma which divides expert opinion. Some questions being asked are, do we irradiate the area where the tumour was, or do we remove that section through surgery."

I was aware of this division of professional opinion but I was already now thinking around these new facts and where I was intending to take this to. Adrian paused and then resumed his professional overview, "My own prejudiced view and based on recent studies where patients with complete responses were left in abeyance and monitored closely, is to do the same. You have no symptoms, there isn't anything to irradiate and that treatment is no free lunch either, there is also nothing to operate on in terms of visible signs. My view is to monitor you aggressively, so a scope every three months and a CT scan every six months with an MRI. Any recurrence we act immediately." I was pleased, this was along the lines of Sami's opinion, that of my oncologist's and the view I had been forming. "I would, however, like you to meet the oncologist here at the QE who is aware of your case, Dr May." I suspected Dr May might be in the other camp, school of thought but he didn't elaborate.

I expressed my thanks for all he had done and was feeling really positive. "Just one question if I may?" I replied tentatively, "How would you describe my journey in medical terms over the course of the last year?"

Adrian thought for a second and responded "You had a stage four tumour/cancer that had spread to other structures in the body, it was a difficult prognosis. Following a complete response to treatment, you have made a remarkable recovery."

I said, "One more thing! I honestly believe my recovery was more than just chemotherapy success, I believe it was a combination of medical but me pushing for the extra antibody drug, pushing the process to its optimum, maximising the medicines in a disciplined structure, having a positive strategy of maximising diet, focuses and self-belief." I think he agreed and disagreed and that was enough for me at that point. My brain was bursting with thoughts, information and I had filled two sides of my pad. After saying my goodbyes and wishing Adrian a good holiday, I returned to my desk, smiling, more confident I was now moving on and found myself staring out of the window next to my desk looking out over the city skyline. I felt powerful and had taken back control of my life.

In the intervening two hours, I phoned my wife and also told a few close friends across a series of texts, phone calls and conversations. Everyone was amazed and happy for me and once I got home after pouring myself a large glass of Merlot, I continued to talk to people, people that had taken an interest in my wellbeing or been thoughtful along the course of journey. Those that appeared to care that is and wanted to communicate with. There were no tears this time, I was happy, strong and moving forward, I had somehow bent the rules or odds, whichever way you looked at it, to end up in a small fortunate minority. I had never doubted it, it had always been my aim and the strategy had delivered. It felt like having scrambled up a mountainside after falling off, having been clinging by fingernails, to have gradually managed to secure footholds, handholds against the buffeting wind, to finally stand on the top of the mountain, upright and surveying the fantastic views of the world around. I thought back to the day I had scaled the side of the bridge on Huntington Lane, a challenge I had overcome. It was the same feeling.

The next day, I penned a list of the people who had been there through the process and made a brief note of how those individuals had been there for me. I had drawn huge positivity from people around me and some had really risen to the occasion. I would always remember them how thoughtful they had been and knew I would be there for them. I was loving the world, I wanted more excitement from it, more high jinx moments perhaps and more family time, to see my kids grow into fine young men and have families of their own.

I texted my chemo nurse, Karen:

Me: "Hi, Karen, just thought I would let you know I beat this! A complete response. Thanks for all your help along the way – Stanley."

Karen: "Bloody fantastic news (grinning face emoji). I'm so chuffed for you and the family, might catch up with you guys by the footy pitch when the boys start the season again (grinning face emoji)."

Me: "Yes, Footie pitch. Thanks, Karen, you made chemo and Certaximab a very easy process."

Chapter 37
A New Day, a New Dawn

On 2nd August, I had diarised a telephone appointment with Jen, my nutritionist, at 5:30 p.m., I had been looking forward to telling her my news and praise the contribution I believed diet had made to my recovery. Before the call, I met Larry for a catch up over a drink. Larry had been down, bouts of depression but was as usual putting a brave face on things. Everything in Larry's life seemed perfect, he had now an established girlfriend who was delivering in all departments, they had just been on a romantic trip to Paris and she seemed to match Larry in terms of sex life demands, even having surprised Larry with what she was prepared to commit to in the Paris hotel room. I still think he was missing his ex and was still meeting her for a liaison, at her request. I was never going to judge Larry but whilst he should be happy, he wasn't, despite having the best of both worlds. We talked about alcohol a bit, Larry thought it created an imbalance which prompted his negative thoughts and depression. I thought it might be. For me, it was good to take my mind off things, I was getting right back to my old self and putting the cancer to the back of my mind, I was, however, living life differently now, a day at a time, spending it wisely and in a way, I wished. Time was now a precious commodity.

I had time for Larry, his chats during my illness had been the perfect tonic and he was a colourful character, rich in the spectrum of life's rich tapestry of experience. Larry talked about leaving his job, getting a barge and with his guitar and girlfriend living a life of hobos, moving from place to place, sex hungry nomads, with the occasional Rolling Stones tune on the guitar. It sounded idyllic but I knew, with the depression, it would not solve Larry's issues. I concluded we all have something in our lives and we are all made so differently psychologically. I had been there for Larry too but I needed to desperately recharge my batteries and get away from things myself. Not for long but right away. I needed retail therapy too, I wanted to spend money now, on things I wanted to.

At 5:30 p.m., as planned, Jen had called me, she was as expected over the moon for me but as confident as ever then delivered the reality check. "You must remember, Stanley, your body allowed this to happen and you don't have nine lives!"

...It took me a few seconds to absorb that statement. Jen went on, expressing assertiveness and authority in her voice, "You have been given another opportunity, this last year has been your tap on the shoulder. In my experience, when it comes back it comes back with vengeance and you have an opportunity to act now to prevent it coming back and to live life to the full. You must treat this as a reminder to self, do everything to adopt the right approach to wellness." I felt a bit sullen and that a stillness in the wind I had been sailing with had momentarily let my sails flap loosely in the calm. We then talked about which bits of the diet I had been sticking to (I was myself impressed, as was she) but still, there was clearly more I could be doing and my diet plan would need to change to fit the new status of post operation, new liver and trying to continue to deliver good results for the scan.

Jen asked me about any pain and I referred to an old back injury associated with my sciatic joint and toenail discolouring which stemmed from my sporting days, my feet being punished inside hockey Astro turf boots week in, week out. Jen pointed to the fact this type of joint inflammation could be a driver for cancer and any nail fungus related issues also came from the gut. For the joint issue, she was keen to recommend an osteopath, to get my joint as flexible and as fluid as possible. I agreed, it all made a lot of sense to me.

We went on to some of the new things that would be important to my recovery. Jen wanted me to take on new supplements to aid the body, it had been a significant period that it had been bombarded with poisons from the treatment drugs, radiation from scans, injections, antibiotics for the acne and a major incision and removal of part of a major organ. Jen would prescribe from the natural dispensary, milk thistle to give my liver support on a long-term basis and to help counteract the effects of alcohol. I had told Jen I would be drinking again albeit sensibly. I would also be put on a three-month course of probiotics, apparently beneficial bacteria, there would be three different types. I would also be on three different types of antioxidants like licapine found in tomatoes. I would be continuing with kapparest to tackle the joint inflammation. To tie in with my medical three monthly testing, Jen wanted me to start functional testing with her, mainly stool and urine samples. This was to look at what caused it and drove the perpetuation of the disease. In Jen's mind, we would pre-empt any imbalances, undo damage, ascertaining and preventing along the way. I was on board, I now had a set of processes to follow, another set of drills to abide by which could save my life. I was happy, Jen was an important ally in the fight against a rogue enemy, we needed to sure up our defences.

The Friday of that week, we went over to Liam and Nina's for supper, we had a lift the short distance up the lane, slowly weaving through the electric gates and crunching along the sweeping gravel drive. It was fantastic food and after, between four of us, drinking a few bottles of champagne and wine I ended up feeling so relaxed and happy. The next morning, I had my first hangover for a long-time. I had forgotten how much a hangover hurt, that throbbing pain in my head, the dryness in my mouth and the lethargic effect of the alcohol. I got out of bed at 1:30 p.m. that day. I felt freedom, a burden had been lifted.

Tuesday, 8th August, I was sat poolside at the Pastana Resort Hotel, Porto Santo, sun rays bursting through the pockets of clouds, my pale skin feeling a different type of radiation, nature's biggest heater. We had flown to the Portuguese island the night before direct from Birmingham, looking forward to our first real holiday in two years, last summer's, of course, having had to be cancelled. I was starting to look back at what had been an incredible journey, all the needles, biopsies, nurses, doctors, operating theatres and drugs. That was over, for now at least and this holiday represented getting back to normal. I was scrolling my phone, messages had died down since my recovery had been announced, people were rightly getting on with their lives too. I wished a friend happy birthday on Facebook, powered up my Lenovo Yoga and started writing some of my diary/book. I was still finding it a good way of getting things/emotion out of my system. When I went into the hotel a few hours later for some refreshments, I noticed a picture of a beach hanging on the wall of a small shop mainly selling branded hotel items. The picture was a photo of a beach with a family walking along it into the sunset. It suddenly occurred to me. This journey was similar to taking a photo. I had needed to focus on what mattered, capturing the positives, learning and moving on from the negatives and being ready for the next shot.

Chapter 38
Emotional Rollercoaster

With the absorption of the news that I was recovered, that I needed no further operations and simply needed to be monitored, the intensity of medical attention ceased apart from the odd letter booking me in for a three monthly review and confirmation letters from my medical provider that such and such invoice had been paid. I started to feel I could get back to normal and the holiday had certainly helped with that and of course being able to drink again.

It was, however, suddenly an emotional time, I hadn't anticipated I would feel like this at all. Part of me (somewhere deep inside my mind and driven by my inner soul), was now realising the consequences of beating the illness having cheated a prognosis of death and what if I hadn't pushed for my medical back in Feb 2016? I wouldn't be here. I should surely be experiencing the ultimate positive wave of energy resulting from having been released to freedom from a situation akin to a self-confined prison cell and life long sentence. But here I was wanting to simply curl up on my own in a ball and cry. It was unbelievable to have been so full of positive energy and then to suddenly experience so many tear jerking moments. I had to treat this as another challenge and it was one of the hardest, there was nothing I could do physically other than exercise, rest and eat good nutritional meals, this was more the mental challenge a by-product of the journey to date. In my mind, I challenged myself to overcome this, trying all ways to flick the switch to positive trying to look at the matter from different angles.

My body was making a great recovery from the operation, the hours of poisons infused into my veins and gradually, the emotion started to seem less day by day, I busied myself with work, a new car and DIY, trying to surround myself with positive people and energy.

Just before I was diagnosed with cancer, my wife had seen a consultant about a fibroid growth outside of her womb. It was clear at the time that this was something which would need removal through surgery, not immediately but in the near future. As a result of what I had been going through medically, my wife applied a selfless kindness in putting me first. Therefore, booking in for an operation to sort herself out wasn't considered by Claudia until my recovery had been confirmed.

It wasn't until late October 17, that I found myself with Claudia sat opposite a formidable and scary female surgeon specialising in fibroids. The message was clear, this fibroid was now huge and needed an immediate removal, it had been left too long. There was no denying that, I had been undergoing treatment for over a year, during that time, the fibroid was growing and had reached such a size it was now degenerating. Within a week, I walked into another hospital, this time in Solihull, Claudia booked in that afternoon for an operation to remove the fibroid. It was a strange feeling being back in the hospital, the gowns, stockings before an operation, the blood tests, blood pressure tests, questionnaires, noises, smells and of course the waiting.

When I finally walked with Claudia to the operating theatre later that day, it was again a very strange feeling, it was the reverse of my experiences over the last year. I was now the person supporting someone else experiencing a medical issue that involved surgery. I walked back from saying my goodbyes to the now empty private room, the bed having been wheeled to theatre and sat in a chair in silence, feeling numb. I tried to write some of my book but couldn't concentrate and texted a few close friends, but it seemed like an eternity of waiting, it felt horrible. An operation scheduled for one and a half hours with one surgeon due to complications took two surgeons and was a long procedure, three hours in total and Claudia was quite poorly in her immediate recovery when they wheeled her back to the room, her slight frame shaking from the anaesthetic, invasive procedures and substantial painkillers kicking in. Claudia looked awful. The fibroid surgeon had needed a second surgeon as the main fibroid, was one of three and weighed in at 3 lbs. It had moved kidneys and other organs due to its position. As a result, the operation was complex and if it hadn't been performed at the fibroid clinic with a second surgeon on standby would have been a risk to her safety.

As I found myself this time on the other side of the fence, rushing frantically to her bedside at all hours, it brought back the same processes I had endured, it was very odd watching someone else go through it. Just being in a hospital, made me think too much about what I had been through, all the machines monitoring rhythms and drip stands, wires and beeps, brought back the experiences at a time I personally needed to think about something else. I felt like I was smothering, suffocating, I suddenly wanted to be anywhere away from hospitals and people.

This is where you need to adapt as a person, use inner strength to keep on the correct path, no matter how hard that might be. I needed to be strong for Claudia who desperately needed me and the kids to support her. Over the next few weeks, Claudia started to progress her recovery, it was a big scar from the incision, the process was slow, it takes time and we worked as a team to work through it.

Inside of me, I knew that time is the great healer, this issue would simply need time to get completely back to where I was pre diagnosis. Would I ever be exactly the same person? The answer to that I knew immediately, 'absolutely not!', I was now wired differently but aside from the stressful emotion of someone else being in hospital now full of a new kind of energy. There was so much I wanted to achieve in life still, things I wanted to see and people I wanted to spend time with.

Here was my new dawn.

Chapter 39
A Day at a Time

In some ways, it was as if I had never had cancer. Here I was again sat opposite Larry in our usual public house, this time each with a beer, talking about fast cars and motor bikes. I told him that I hoped to be acquiring another sports car this time a BMW M4 and Larry told me he was adding to his collection of amazing old motorcycles which he was busy restoring himself. This time, he was buying an old Norton that needed a lot of work. Larry also enlightened me on his quest to find a third female interest, this time perhaps someone in the building where he worked, where mutual interest in a mid-morning workout may provide an alternative to burning calories in the gym. I chuckled, grinning at the thought of Larry propositioning women in the queue for the photocopier.

It was November 17 and I had just finished part of what I saw as a three-point process. The last part of the process was a full abdomen, chest and pelvis CT scan, this had followed bloods being taken to check my CEA score (measuring cancer proteins) and a few weeks before the scan, a day case operation, being put back into theatre and asleep so they could go looking for any sign of nodes or cancer with a full colonoscopy. In essence, this was my first MOT. I was at the key three-month point.

Prior to this point, I had been getting into life's routine again, forgetting about my journey to date, bouncing back to life, left alone and whilst I kept the food diet, I was back to drinking, things were as normal as possible. It was as though I had never had cancer, I felt great.

As Larry described the type of female he was looking for, who sounded half his age and would still need to have an interest in confectionary, I knew I was back in a waiting game, as Larry spoke his words drifting over me, it came back to me the long periods of not knowing I had endured, the endless chasing of the surgeon's secretary or texting my busy oncologist for an update. Larry was now describing his latest bout of depression and at his lowest point, recently had thought about ending his life. I heard that bit and responded with positive vibes, trying to understand his mind-set but not succeeding very well, my mind was elsewhere. Ironically, here was a guy who with all the sex and mars bars in the world, would take a chance to end his life, sat opposite him me, a guy determined to save my life at all costs.

Fuck, I thought, *this is another big milestone...would this three month MOT be good news or bad.* Feeling great is one thing, but at the back of your mind is the fact that something caused my cells to break down in the first place, this could happen again. What had caused my cancer was impossible to know.

All you can do is take it a day at a time, stay positive and most of all, totally focused, I imagine this pressure for some people would send you mad. I needed Larry to keep me distracted and as I listened to his list of potential female partakers, I smiled, I needed to just relax, listen to Larry and all would be fine with my results. If it wasn't, I would simply do everything possible to beat the next process and the next.

In the next few days, I left messages for the surgeon's secretary about any news on my results, I was always polite as was she but as the days went past, there was nothing to report back to me and each time whilst I became more anxious, I felt for her having to deal with people like me daily just wanting to know news critical to their situation. Ten days had now gone past since my scan, your mind races thinking 'there must be something wrong for it to take this long', the other side of my brain was saying you are fine, look at you, you're feeling fit and healthy.

Finally, the call came from Sue, Adrian's secretary, there were no signs of residual cancer or nodes on the scan or from the scope, my first three-month scan was an all-clear. I was overjoyed, massively relieved and it felt like a weight had been lifted. In many ways, this welcome news helped me with the emotional journey, I was getting on with things and this recovery wasn't just a flash in the pan, every day was a bonus. I phoned Larry on the car phone back from work and told him how precious life was and how positive I felt.

Chapter 40
An Unusual Christmas

The operation Claudia had had in October, had left her with a stent between the kidney and the bladder, this was left in situ for six weeks and came out 8th December, under a local anaesthetic, we travelled home the same day that the stent was removed. That evening, Claudia was violently sick, had uncontrollable shivers and I ended up on the phone to the ward that had discharged her all through the night. Neither of us got any sleep. Claudia didn't eat most of the weekend and was bed ridden. The days that followed, Claudia felt queasy and ate very little but in some ways, it seemed part of the recovery process, certainly according to the ward that was their perception.

By Wednesday, I took her to her GP, who immediately diagnosed a urine infection and prescribed an oral antibiotic. Claudia's colour seemed more greyish and we booked to see the consultant who had performed the operation on the Friday at the fibroid clinic. They again tested urine and this time bloods too, they were concerned Claudia had lost weight. My father had acted as chauffeur that day and after the tests, dropped me at the local train station so I could get a lift into work, my last official day until the office reopened after the Christmas break on 2nd January.

The day was normal enough, I finished my work, had a beer or two and lunch with the team members who were left and then bought a few last minute presents at the House of Fraser. It was when I got home at 7:30 that evening the next medical roller coaster started.

Claudia's consultant had phoned half an hour earlier to report the bloods and urine tests pointed to a serious infection now affecting Claudia's kidney and given that the private hospitals were not taking admissions this close to Christmas, to go to A&E. By 8:30 p.m., we were both waiting in A&E to see a doctor. This took time, we were first seen by a paramedic at 10 p.m., then eventually a doctor by 11 p.m. who took new bloods for testing. We waited endlessly in a treatment room until the doctor came back saying he just saw the results as part of the healing procedure from the operation. I complained and told him to speak to Claudia's consultant and that this was more serious. At 1:00 a.m., we were seen by another doctor responsible for medical admissions, who agreed Claudia needed to be admitted immediately and that a CT scan needed to be undertaken Saturday morning. At 2:00 a.m., I left Claudia on a ward, the intravenous drip being administered to combat the infection. Claudia looked exhausted.

The next morning, I hadn't slept but got back to the hospital. Large parts of the hospital were shutting down ready for Christmas, and they were in 'go slow' mode. The scan, however, was undertaken and showed a swollen kidney not draining properly, the stent removal had somehow caused an obstruction, the kidney would become infected as it was full of urine.

I started to raise the stakes with calls and texts to Claudia's consultant and the medical insurer, nothing seemed to be happening and Christmas with the kids at home was just around the corner, or was it? A private hospital seemed out of the question. On the Sunday, we were told they would be moving Claudia to Heartlands Hospital in Birmingham, by ambulance, I followed by car shortly afterwards. The move was necessary so Claudia could be treated in a major hospital where teams were still working over the Christmas break. The idea being, a stent could be reinserted to allow the kidney to drain properly. I found myself travelling on Christmas Eve back to Birmingham and then on Christmas day itself they went in through Claudia's back to drain the kidney, a tube draining urine to a small external bag by her side. The antibiotics were working, her colour came back but she was still underweight and resigned to her bed. At some point Claudia would need a stent fitted and the drain taken out. I was annoyed we were both missing a normal Christmas but it is a set of processes you just have to get through and you can't foresee or pick the timing of life's big events. Not a lot happened the next few days, I would visit daily, making the six-hour round trip, enjoying the drive in the BMW M4. I imagined other families enjoying their Christmas breaks with their families and tried to make the boys have a great Christmas while I was around.

The ward Claudia was on was dated, old school NHS. Six beds with all female patients of various ages, and the loo and showers were in the corridor. The hospital was a busy and reflected Birmingham's multi-cultural community, with many different conversations going on around you in different languages.

We amused ourselves with the observations around us. One day, I was sat in the armchair, Claudia in the bed when a little old man, perhaps late 80s or early 90s, shuffled along the corridor, he was a visitor dressed in his Sunday best. Suddenly, Rihanna's *'Like a Diamond'* erupted in a loud ring tone from his coat pocket but which one, it took him a long time to locate the phone. We chuckled, such a trendy mobile ring tone so loud.

In the bed next to Claudia was a large woman again in her 80s, a Glaswegian with six chins, lying mainly prostate, her loose pink nightie covering her bulky frame. At regular intervals, she would complain with a curse. One physio suggested she should go for a gentle walk unaided to the loo. "Fuck off, am I doing that!" came the quick response in a thick Glaswegian accent. "I fucking can't even wipe my own arse!"

Another time, the nurse arrived to her bedside and said, "I have a pot here with a large number of pills I need you to take, I just need to wet your lips." The nurse gently leaned into Carol and wiped Carol's lips, placing the full paper pot of pills on the moveable table which was positioned over the bed. As she leaned back up, the nurse looked shocked as Carol suddenly grabbed the pot and tried to swallow all of the pots contents in one go.

"Uh…all in one go is fine…" The nurse was still in shock, most of the multi-coloured pills now hanging from Carol's wetted lips, some stuck to her tongue, others gently wobbling in the air then falling gracefully to the starched bed sheet below. It was impossible not to laugh at the struggle the nurse was having getting Carol to do any simple task.

It was on the next occasion that I visited Claudia at Heartlands, when from the other side of the curtain which separated Claudia and Carol came a massive splatter sound, like someone dropping a bucket of soup from height on the smooth hard floor.

"Ah. Fuck…nurse…ah, fuck…nurse…it's me bag, Nurse, me bag has burst!"

"Hold your nose," I told Claudia , as a deep unsettling smell of stale urine wafted quickly to our side of the curtain and the nurse first on the scene was stunned, even managing an expressively felt 'Shit!' statement before calling for backup. Carol had leaned on her colostomy bag and given her weight it had split sending the contents of the sack in all directions, over Carol, over the floor, the bed and the wall. I felt for the nurses, they were clearly run off their feet and being pulled in all directions with limited resource.

Somehow, despite not wanting Claudia to be in hospital as the days went on, my mental attitude emerged from wanting to be anywhere else but a hospital to seeing it as a rough kind of therapy. It was helping me put my own experience in perspective, although I was frustrated by the slow pace of the NHS system, Claudia's procedure delayed, then delayed again.

On 28th December, Claudia went back to theatre to have a new stent and the kidney drain removed. It is a strange sensation going to see someone on a ward of six beds and finding only five on arrival, the patient and bed you are meant to be visiting gone, just an open space of hospital floor. I had been too late arriving to wish her well, I would need to be there on her return to the ward.

The procedure had gone well this time and on the 30th, Claudia was told she would be discharged and at 11 a.m., I was there ready to take her home. The system couldn't cope though, the doctor would have to write a discharge letter and then the nurse review the paperwork, they had no time to do these tasks. I heard other patients asking for discharge letters too, languishing in their aged hospital beds, gradually getting more and more impatient.

I asked both doctors and nurses if we could go but it was 5 p.m. when we finally got the all clear some six hours later. I felt I should be cross but you can't be, these doctors and nurses are literally working flat out, long hours, I admired their sheer commitment to their duties and appreciated even more how I had been looked after by all sorts of medical staff in the process of my treatment whilst I was ill. It felt wonderful walking out of a hospital after eight days of visiting, I wanted it to be sometime before anyone I knew was hospitalised. I wanted 2018 to be a better year for that outlook.

Chapter 41
March 2018

It had been a difficult few months with Claudia's hospitalisation and finally in February after having her stent successfully removed during an operation to balloon the damaged tube between the kidney and bladder, she was given the all clear and we started to get back to normality. It was hard mentally, I could feel the emotion and a pressure now and then. I could find myself in networking events where I just needed to get out, to breathe, I felt claustrophobic, my mind was telling me, look what you came through, it's been circa two years of hospitals, intensive care, operations, now you just have to get back into your routine life. Occasionally, I would feel a powerful rise from within of pure emotion sometimes the odd tear. I would often try and escape be on my own or go to a safe place where I was happy.

More and more, I felt that I needed to get away on my own and soon. I decided on a ski trip to Italy, a small town called Madessimo hidden high in the Italian Dolomites, I had been many years before and loved it then, I hoped it wouldn't disappoint. I mentioned my intended trip to Larry, Digger, Chet and TJ on separate occasions and before I knew it they were all coming with me, booking in to stay at the same small family run hotel. I was, in some ways, reluctant to have lots of pals around me but on reflection I saw it as a massive positive and started to really look forward to it more and more. Besides, I was there for seven days with TJ, Digger would be there for five days and Chet and Larry would come out for four days, we would be flying to Italy from different airports.

The day before I was scheduled to fly out from Bristol to Bergamo (Northern Milan), I was at Cheltenham festival with pals from the office, drinking fine wine, great company and I felt so relaxed. I had to literally drag myself away from the clutches of temptation levied by my companions to stay and drink, party on. As it was, I stuck to my plan and got home at a reasonable hour to put the finishing touches to my packing. TJ picked me up early before 7 a.m. and we were off, off on a new adventure, space and escaping nothing specific but a weight was lifting off my mind. I needed to think through what I was going through.

On the private transfer from Bergamo to Madessimo, I loved just looking out of the car window, the different styles of architecture, streetscapes and jaw dropping mountains as we started our incline past Lake Como's vast length and snaking the steep narrow roadways and through tunnels towards Madessimo. It was the peaceful beautiful mountain retreat out of school season that I remembered, with its pure mountain air and surrounded by stunning mountains tree lined with pine forests and magical whiteness of deep snow brightening to the eye, everywhere.

Sadly for Digger, relationship issues back home confined much of his trip to his room, he had no appetite for food, skiing, sleep or drinking, he looked awful. We were supportive and got him skiing a few times but I also needed to focus on me and my journey through the mire of emotional feeling. As the large characters of Larry and Chet had yet to arrive, TJ and I found ourselves skiing from 9 a.m. to 11 a.m. most days, having a few beers, then skiing until lunch with usually a generous pizza with more beer, continuing to ski until 4 p.m. where we would have another beer before hitting the hotel for a shower. We would get changed and go out for another few beers before the hotel set menu meeting Digger and heading out again. It sounds like we would be hammered by that point but it was a nice pace and we talked so much. TJ knew me so well and it was what I needed, I was downloading day by day. I loved it.

Larry and Chet arrived on the Sunday, there they sat in the hotel's bar comfy chairs smiling with their beers. It was good to see them, I wondered how Larry would cope with the Italian women and whether his infamous charm offensive would have the same success as in the UK.

The group dynamic changed when they arrived, there was less time to download to TJ but we would ski as a group, sometimes, Digger would venture out of his room to join us for a few hours and then disappear, it worked well.

I found that something about me was, indeed, different post recovery, when we were out skiing one day. The five of us had skied a long way without a break and stopped half-way down a steep red which overlooked a long straight blue track leading to a distant ski lift. We concluded that with only the occasional turn on the red slope, we could each set off then put the skis completely straight pointing downhill and be in a fast tuck position skiing without any traversing to the ski lift. In doing so, we would test out a new ski app which measured speed, distance, altitude along with other things like degree of slope. The higher up the red you were and the straighter you pointed your skis downhill, would give you the higher speed.

TJ went first and when we met at the bottom had clocked an impressive 34 miles per hour, "Beat that, lads, it felt really quick!" I could feel the competitiveness rising within me, I desperately wanted to beat that time, I feared nothing. The game continued all day, we would reach a steep straight red slope and go straight down without turning from the highest point of the slope we felt comfortable with. I would point out that this was using Italian hire equipment too, very risky, we had no downhill racing skis or boots. The timings were creeping up, I clocked a 44 mph, then TJ a 47 mph.

When TJ clocked a 51 mph he calmly said, "Look, enough is enough, that was proper shit your pants stuff, let's call it a day." When one of Britain's leading bomb disposal operators says he was scared, it was dangerous.

"Let me have one more run," I said, "I am afraid of nothing!"

Larry and Chet tried to talk me out of it, Digger said it was pointless but TJ said, "All right but only if you are sure?" I was.

I found a point 600m up the red slope, turned downhill and just went low into an immediate tuck pushing all my weight into my shins and stretching my poles out over the front of my skis. The wind started racing past my crash helmet and I felt my velocity increasing, it felt so fast, faster than I had ever been on skis in my life. My helmet started to lift at the front, its strap trying to strangle me but I kept going, just a few seconds longer could make the difference. Stopping was hard at that speed, I had less room than I thought as everything was happening so quickly, I forced a huge parallel turn cascading a huge cloud of powder at the bottom of the slope in all directions, it helped kill some of the speed, I came to a halt some 15 meters further on. My heart was pounding through my chest, my mouth dry. As I turned to get the phone out of my pocket and give it to TJ who was waiting nearby, he looked at me and said, "Fucking hell, Stanley, enough, you did 54.7 mph and I am not even going to try and beat that."

We found a few new bars on the ski slopes too, one in particular was slightly off the main routes, it always just seemed to be us in there, strange compilation of music too, sometimes 90s love songs other times yodelling hits! It had military memorabilia in cases dotted around the wooden chalet-style wall panels. The bar staff were female, one about Larry's age, and a glint of mischief in her eye. I suspected she spent most of her time on her own waiting for the rare customer or group when it wasn't height of season.

I think it was the next day, we were mid-ski when Larry piped up, "Sorry, lads…I think I have a mild case of the shits…I think I will head down to that bar and chill out for a bit!" Initially, I felt sorry for Larry as he skied off in a different direction towards the bar, I also wondered what music they would be playing today, some cowboy compilation I imagined. It was about ten minutes later, I realised this was Larry's play for an Italian woman, to see if that really was a glint in her eye. I smiled as I pictured Larry using his pigeon Italian to tell her he liked her music compilations, would prefer her to serve him drinks naked and to put the 'closed for business' sign on the door for a few hours.

On speaking to Larry later that day, I wasn't far off the mark in my thinking, unfortunately, however, Larry's plan started to unravel shortly after arriving at the bar. The sultry Italian was alone and flirting back as Larry sat enjoying his beer, commenting on the Second World War artefacts, then on her cute looks. This took Larry much longer than usual, the language barrier disrupting his well-drilled smooth patter of edgy suggestive compliments. Larry had, by that point of the play, got up and moved closer to the bar, starting to use his tactile approach to break down any language issues. It was at that point, to Larry's dismay, the owner of the bar, an Italian serving sergeant, arrived with all his army mates. Larry had to make a sharp exit, heading back to the hotel to only imagine what could have been the most pleasurable of afternoons off piste.

The trip was good for me, I could have stayed longer, I was relaxed and on form looking forward not back. Larry seemed in a good place too, always smiling and displaying the confident red-blooded male character that he was.

Chapter 42
The Crematorium

Not long after returning to the UK, Claudia's father, having recently past his 80th birthday, died in his bed at the nursing home where he resided, suffering from dementia. Suddenly, our lives were upside down again, with lots to sort out and of course, Claudia needing my support as she dealt with the emotional rollercoaster a daughter feels in losing a father unexpectedly. I tried my best to be there but I was still coping with getting to grips with my own recent experience. In amongst this new episode of drama, I was due to have my next round of tests, a scope, CT scan and blood tests to see if the cancer had returned.

The scope operation in April at the private hospital in Birmingham, I didn't mind, I had no fear of being put to sleep while they explored my bowel in high definition. I looked forward to the day, it was even good to catch up with the medical staff, many of whom I had met through previous procedures. The CT scan was the same, a few days later, I found myself again sat in a gown, drinking metallic tasting fluids which would light up my insides but I was happy, I looked forward to the experience.

It was, however, the waiting that followed that was hard to deal with, I had got used to my life again free from external control, suddenly being in a medical process again and having to play the waiting game was a pressure. It took about two weeks to finally receive a letter confirming that there was no sign of reoccurring or residual cancer. I was happy but I could feel that pressure of emotion or claustrophobia.

The private family service at the crematorium for Claudia's father was hard. Josh stayed with my parents, we simply took the view he was too young to deal with seeing the coffin disappear behind a set of curtains. Flynn, my eldest son, whilst nearly 15, was very emotional through the service and outside. I found myself sitting with him on a quiet bench nestled in-between the tranquil, carefully manicured landscaped borders surrounding the crematorium, Flynn sobbing into my handkerchief. I was there for Flynn at that point, my own feelings just seemed to be a numbness. In the following church service where my wife and her sisters all partook in a moving eulogy, Josh, who had joined us, was the one to cry from that part of the service. I moved rows across the church to be with him, putting my arm around his shoulders offering him only a tissue, my handkerchief still being with Flynn. Small pieces of wet tissue gathered on the floor at his feet as he sobbed. I noticed that some of my relatives were sobbing too, two of my aunties had travelled from Cardiff to offer their support for Claudia, they didn't really know her father but sat there in their black clad outfits, tears in their eyes, mascara staining their eyelids. I felt only numbness.

The next morning, my dad drove me to the train station, I had something on at work where I needed a lift. I commented how strange it was that my aunts were crying.

"It was emotional for all of us, Stanley," he said seriously, "in many ways, a lot of us thought that they would have had to attend your funeral when you were given your initial prognosis."

I sat there knowing I had thought the same when I had been supporting my boys at the funeral, wondering how they would have been if I hadn't beaten the illness. I felt emotional but I felt strong, I felt I had beaten death.

Chapter 43
The Golden Orb

Initially, I had no intention of writing this chapter as I felt it would seem somewhat unbelievable but it is perhaps wrong to leave it out given I had a complete response to treatment, a rare thing and I cannot categorically attribute my full recovery to one single thing. I am not religious, I went to church and Sunday school as a kid but God doesn't make any sense to me with the destruction, poverty and cruelty in the world. That said, people I know wanted to pray for me while I was ill, a Catholic church in the Cotswolds holding a mass for me, a Chistadelphian Church group in Worcestershire praying for me regularly and of course, my mum and dad's Methodist church in Hereford. In addition, a guy in my team prayed for me every Friday lunchtime at the Birmingham Central Mosque. Personally, I was aware of it, supported their caring thoughts and welcomed it. It was after all a positive.

If I am honest, I had a moment or two where I asked a higher something to change my circumstances, if you are dying I think a lot of you would. I don't think I was praying to God, my own interpretation is that there is a lot in cosmology and looking towards the stars, a higher being and asking for some things in life does work. You sometimes just need to be able to deal with the consequences and be careful for what you ask. I had asked the Cosmos to allow me to survive.

On this one evening in late 2016, I was in my bedroom, getting ready for bed. I had cleaned my teeth, was sat in boxers and a t-shirt, and my wife was doing something in the spare room. Suddenly, what I can only describe as a golden orange orb, roughly the size of a small grapefruit, travelled through the window and curtain at speed, without damaging anything and landed on the bed next to me. Without a moment's hesitation, I ran as fast as I could towards Claudia shouting, "Quick, you have to see this…what just happened!"

Claudia ran back with me down the narrow landing corridor, arriving with me in the doorway asking with nervous energy, "What happened, what just happened?"

There was nothing on the bed, no damaged curtains or windows, and I tried explaining it in detail to Claudia, who just looked at me in supportive amazement, eventually going back to the spare room.

The weird thing was, I felt its energy, whatever it was, it had power and I thrived on energy, I took it as a sign of something, maybe a helping hand from the stars, a God or our maker. I will never know the answer, but it is how you use an experience like that, let it give you more fight and more purpose.

Chapter 44
The X Factor

Looking back, I had a well-thought out, polished strategy to tackle cancer. I was in good physical shape going into this sequence of events and I was mentally up for a challenge, taking the diagnosis, treatment and changes in my life, in my stride. However, the point about being inspired to be brave, to fight, to want to win, to believe comes from somewhere deep within the soul, that is something unique to all of us and is an X factor ingredient. That looking forward to something, someone or someones, beyond the life changing event that confronts you, that strong love of something or persons in your life could be the differential, it can itself be so powerful. That longing to achieve success, driven by a motivation built on a love of something in life is a special thing and something to be nurtured always. It is the biggest weapon in your armoury.

Since getting the all clear, people come up to me and tell me about people they know on receiving a diagnosis, letting cancer simply control them or accepting death, not wanting to put up a fight. Others binge eating to combat the negativity and depression so often associated with cancer but eating the wrong foods encouraging their cancer cells to grow. I have the same message for all of them…be inspired to fight it, life is wonderful even if you extend it by a few days, weeks, months or years, it is so worth it, life is an amazingly beautiful and precious thing.

I was feeling so good, positive, healthy, alive, a weight had been lifted and now I was feeling it. Every moment was so precious, breathing air was a celebration with each breath, staring at birds, trees and the clear blue sky a joy. I felt a huge amount of gratitude for those who had helped me and out of the list of those who had supported me, there were a few who had gone even further, over and beyond the level of great caring friends who as you would expect to regularly call, text and/or visit. These few had been in regular contact like everyone else but had been in addition so thoughtful, delivered worthwhile solid advice at key times or nuggets of gold contributing to the battle plan. Their intent on wanting to stop what they were doing to think about me and get involved meant a huge amount and in some cases, I genuinely think made the difference.

There was, of course, my wife, Claudia, how would I have coped without her, doing everything possible to manage the household, keep the normality around the kids during my treatment, ensuring we maximised the medication with detailed plans for all tablets, accompanying me to incredibly difficult meetings with consultants and holding my hand before I was operated on and then when I came out of surgery. Rearranging my whole diet in line with Jen, the nutritionist's recommendations, making the absence of refined sugar, dairy, bread, alcohol and the addition of foods like turmeric seem so easy, through hard work preparing meals in the kitchen. Claudia's love and support was always there throughout the process along with my two fabulous boys and my dog, Skyla, lying at my feet throughout my chemo.

On the list of other people who ventured above and beyond, whether they in fact knew it or not were the following people. There was Carl and my boss, Jason, from my department at work, one who had instigated the other's recommendation of the antibody drug and told me about his dad's friend's experience

217

with the same condition and that I should mention it to my oncologist. I know, as a fact, my oncologist wasn't going to raise it with me and if Carl had not mentioned this drug, I may not be where I am now. In my view, a game changer.

Then there was Nina, who I had only known a few years and yet, from the very start, pushed me towards, Jen the nutritionist, relating her own experiences to me and nutrition with such relevance. I would never have embraced nutrition as part of the fight without Nina and this early intervention early in the process was a game changer too.

Digger was another, phoning me literally every day or taking me out for drives before major treatment, building me a mancave and helping me buy a classic car to take my mind off things. Digger had an empire of 800 people to run but was often driving a 60-mile round trip to mow my lawns or clean out my garage. These focuses were a game changer.

I couldn't have done this journey anywhere near as well without Claudia or the above people making key differences along the way, interventions or amazing support. There was, of course, my parents, my dad acting as my chauffeur and constantly doing jobs in the garden or doing a multitude of jobs around the house. My mum was the same, making foods specific to my diet plan or regularly helping with things like looking after and feeding the kids while we were at hospital and keeping me stocked up with a regular supply of Manuka honey. My mother-in-law also helped with those times when my wife and I were at hospital appointments.

A special thanks goes to the many surgeons, medical teams, nurses and all those dedicated NHS, private hospital staff and chemo nurses. I would not be here without their input. I most certainly would not be here without Sami, my liver surgeon, Adrian, my bowel surgeon and their fantastic teams, their professionalism and supportive positivity was faultless.

Of course, where also would I have been without Larry? Where would I be without so many great people around me?